99YARNS and Counting

MORE DESIGNS FROM THE GREEN MOUNTAIN SPINNERY

99 YARNS and Counting

MORE DESIGNS FROM THE GREEN MOUNTAIN SPINNERY

The Green Mountain
Spinnery Cooperative

Photography by Marti Stone

THE COUNTRYMAN PRESS
WOODSTOCK, VERMONT

Photographs by Marti Stone
Book design and composition by Eugenie S. Delaney

Published by The Countryman Press,
P.O. Box 748, Woodstock, VT 05091

Distributed by W. W. Norton & Company, Inc.,
500 Fifth Avenue, New York, NY 10110

Printed in China

10 9 8 7 6 5 4 3 2 1

This book is dedicated to the earth.

*To the animals and plants that
provide beautiful natural fibers.*

*To the shepherds and growers who tend their
flocks and farms responsibly and humanely.*

*To the venerable mill machinery with
which we transform fiber into yarn.*

*And to you, the knitters and artisans who turn
our yarns into useful and magnificent fabrics.*

Contents

Introduction

The Green Mountain Spinnery has had the good fortune to produce fine natural-fiber yarns and knitting patterns for more than a quarter century. Our first book, *The Green Mountain Spinnery Knitting Book,* included 30 contemporary and classic patterns, to the delight of knitters everywhere. You hold in your hands our second book, in which we've collected another 36 of our favorite patterns.

You'll find in these pages classic, stylish, and fun garments for adults and children. We've included a flock of sweater designs—Arans, raglans, pullovers, and cardigans—as well as shawls, shells, vests, and an array of sock, mitten, and hat patterns. We've even included an afghan we just couldn't resist. Our patterns are designed to bring you joy and satisfaction, and to encourage your own creative adventures in knitting.

Before you begin to knit we'd like to share a bit about our accomplishment in becoming a worker-owned cooperative and take you on a photographic tour of our mill so you can learn more about the yarn-making process. In the end, we want this book to leave you with a full appreciation of the many elements that contribute to the beauty of our yarns, which you transform by the work of your hands.

99 Yarns and Counting

When our first book, *The Green Mountain Spinnery Knitting Book,* came out in 2003, we were on the cusp of what has proven to be a most exciting time for the fiber arts. Hand knitting surged in popularity as young people discovered the joy of creating something beautiful and lasting with their own hands. Lapsed knitters also took up their needles again, spurred by the arrival of grandchildren or a longing for a calmer life. Knitting not only leads to the creation of practical and beautiful fabrics, it is a path to deep reflection and artistic self-expression.

The increase in the popularity of yarn crafts has made the Green Mountain Spinnery a destination for knitters. Visitors to our mill often have very particular expectations. Some expect to find us treadling away on old-fashioned spinning wheels; others expect a slick, modern facility; some even envision sheep grazing on a nearby hillside.

Actually, when you arrive at the Spinnery for a visit, you will open the door into what has been described as the tiniest yarn shop ever. Tiny it may be, but it is a knitter's heaven—packed with natural yarns, patterns galore, and inspiring samples of beautiful finished garments.

Your eyes will be dazzled by the colorful yarns. Your nose will alert you to the blended aroma of sheep grease, machine oil, and steam. Your ears will fill with the rumble of the mill's machinery as workers prepare raw fleece and spin it into yarn.

If you continue on through the tiny store, you'll enter our spinning mill. It is here that we make thousands of pounds of yarn each year for individual farmers, yarn shops, and knitters like you.

A WEB OF MANY YARNS

In 1981, Libby Mills, Claire Wilson, David Ritchie, and Diana Wahle founded the Green Mountain Spinnery based on the principles of E. F. Schumacher's *Small Is Beautiful: Economics as if People Mattered.* In addition to making yarn, their goal was to create a workplace committed to sustainability, to the wise and responsible use of natural resources, and to the support of small-scale farms. Their vision has become reality one step at a time. You can read more stories about our beginnings in *The Green Mountain Spinnery Knitting Book.*

Today the Spinnery's yarn offerings have expanded from its first basic wool yarn in five colors to many fibers, including 34 colors of Mountain Mohair, 20 colors of Wonderfully Woolly, 10 colors of Sylvan Spirit, 14 colors of Cotton Comfort, 5 colors of Yarn Over, 5 colors of Alpaca Elegance, 3 colors of Green Mountain Green, 2 varieties of Spinnery Sock Art, and shades of Vermont, Maine, and New Mexico Organics—99 different yarns in all. (More information about our yarns can be found on page 113).

We select predominantly U.S.-grown fibers for our raw materials. We work closely with fiber producers to help them improve flock management, thus ensuring the availability of high-quality fibers. We pay a fair price, buying as much local and New England–grown fiber as possible. We have used tiny amounts of mohair on occasion from our neighbors in Quebec and Tencel from trees grown in South Africa.

The Spinnery has supported New England's farmers for many years, helping to improve the quality and diversity of local fleece. Coupled with the recent explosion in popularity of fiber crafts is an increase in the

MAKING A NEW YARN

The design of a new yarn may come from an inspiring type of fiber such as local alpaca, superfine kid mohair, or Tencel. Sometimes a customer requests a type of yarn we have never made before. Our Spinnery Sock Art—Meadow was developed after such a request, for a lace weight 2-ply yarn incorporating premium kid mohair.

To design a new yarn we blend small samples of different fiber types and colors on hand cards and spin this up the old-fashioned way, on a spinning wheel. We may try various proportions of fibers and colors, making a number of these small samples until we establish the final "recipe"—a yarn that we think is really exciting.

Claire Wilson, David Ritchie, and Libby Mills, Spinnery Founders

number of "farm yarns" available to knitters. Crafting these exciting custom yarns makes up 60 percent of our mill's production. Yarn styles range from lace weight to bulky and use fleeces from a diversity of sheep breeds, including Cormo, CVM Romeldale, Merino, Romney, Jacob, and Navajo Churro. We have also blended wool with fibers as varied as hemp, silk, angora, llama, and quiviut.

SPINNING INTO THE FUTURE: A COOPERATIVE MILL

One of the Spinnery's founding goals was to create a worker-owned business so that profits from the business would stay with those doing the work. The Spinnery founders always worked collaboratively, sharing the responsibilities of management. They made decisions by consensus, often involving the entire staff.

In 2003, as founders Libby and Claire contemplated retirement, questions about the Spinnery's future surfaced. How would the Spinnery adapt to changing markets? How would it retain its unique vision? How could employees become more involved in the company?

David, the remaining founder, preferred not to be a sole proprietor. This led the founders and staff to further explore the possibilities of cooperative ownership. For two years Stacy Cordiero was our consultant on this transition. Margaret Atkinson, a staff member who became a co-op member, recounts the experience: "It was a challenging process. The workers had so much to learn about the company's finances and its budgeting and planning process. We revised our business plan and personnel policies and grew to understand just how much David, Claire, and Libby had taken on over the years. We also had to keep producing and selling yarns and doing all the daily work. A promising omen at that time was Stacy's surname, Cordiero; it means 'shepherd' in Portuguese."

In November of 2006, six staff members made their final commitment to cooperative ownership of the Spinnery, and a new chapter in the Green Mountain Spinnery's innovative history began. Co-op member Laurie Gilbert says of the transition, "I feel more a part of the place; I know more about the operation of the business financially and have a say in our direction." Co-op member Gail Haines agrees. "Working on developing our skills at making business decisions together takes a lot of time and effort. We still struggle with balancing the need to produce our yarns, which are the core of the business, and making time to meet and work together on decisions, but this is part of what makes this a fun and interesting place to work."

The transition to a worker-owned cooperative allowed Libby and Claire to step away from daily work at the Spinnery while still participating as members of the Cooperative Board of Directors. They know the business will continue with new energy while also remaining true to its founding vision. When customers and farmers communicate with the Spinnery today, we hope our shared enthusiasm is apparent.

A Day's Work at
Green Mountain Spinnery

We welcome visitors and enjoy giving tours of our mill. The following pages give you, the reader, a sense of the process. Transforming raw fleece into yarn involves several steps: scouring, picking, carding, spinning, and finishing. Here is how this happens on a typical weekday at the Green Mountain Spinnery.

A TOUR OF OUR MILL: RAW FLEECE TO SPUN YARN

Tedd or Ingrid—the scouring crew—arrives early and begins to heat water in preparation for washing the wool or other fiber scheduled for processing that day. A "lot" of fiber may be anywhere from 50 pounds to 300 pounds or more, and David will have set out the necessary raw fibers for the scouring crew the night before. Laurie, our mechanic and carder, also arrives early to do general maintenance on the carding machine and prepare it for the day's work.

Scouring begins by soaking fiber in a large sink in very hot soapy water. After soaking, the fiber is moved through a series of squeeze rollers and basins of hot water until it is clean. The wet fiber is then placed in an extractor, the oldest piece of equipment in our mill. Built in 1896 and acquired from the laundry room of the now defunct Windham Hotel in Bellows Falls, Vermont, it is equivalent to the spin cycle of a home washing machine. While the drum spins (and squeals!), a final hot-water rinse is sprayed over the fiber. Once this last water is spun out, the clean fiber is put into an industrial dryer. The scouring process may run from early in the day to late afternoon, depending on lot size.

LANOLIN EXPERIMENTS—SLUDGE INTO GOLD

Lanolin, the natural grease in raw wool, protects both the sheep's skin and its wool. It has been valued by humans for centuries as a healing salve and for use in cosmetics and soaps. Although the Spinnery washes hundreds of pounds of wool a week and filters its wash water to remove the lanolin-rich sludge, we do not produce enough lanolin to interest a large-scale soap or cosmetic company.

Co-op member Patty Blomgren has been experimenting with methods for refining the sludge, which, in addition to lanolin, contains manure and vegetation as well as anything else that came in contact with the sheep. The refining process involves boiling and straining the sludge—a task only for those who can tolerate the smell! Patty uses low-tech methods to keep the process environmentally friendly, as well as inexpensive, and works only with the sludge from our Certified Organic yarns. Patty has been able to purify enough lanolin from the sludge to create several small batches of hand creams.

The Spinnery has begun to offer custom-spinning customers the opportunity to receive their wool sludge back so they can also experiment. As the market for local products grows, another innovative Vermont company might emerge; perhaps our extracted lanolin will find future uses.

Waste water from scouring is heavy with grease and dirt. To minimize its environmental impact we use a unique water filtration system that separates the grease from the dirty water. This lessens the impact on our local sewage system.

The next step is picking. Locks of fiber, still rather densely packed, are opened and blended. Laurie picks the whole lot two or three times. During final picking, fibers are lightly sprayed with spinning oil, which helps them flow through the next steps of processing. Moisture keeps static electricity from building up, preventing the fibers from clumping together and jamming the machines.

Picking is also the step in which different types and colors of fibers are combined. The Spinnery has developed an individual recipe—a mix of natural colored and/or dyed fibers—for each of its 99 yarns. Ingredients for the particular yarn recipe are weighed and layered before being blended in the picker. These yarn recipes allow us to make the same color over and over again, though slight variations in the dyes and fibers create subtle differences between lots.

After final picking, fluffed-up fibers are moved to the 1916 Davis & Furber

carding machine. Picked fiber is added to the feed-box and conveyed to a series of rotating drums that blend the fibers into a web. This is layered into the second half of the carding machine for further blending. Finally the web is separated into pencil roving and wound onto four spools, each holding 24 continuous strands. Although pencil roving looks like yarn, it has neither twist nor tensile strength.

The spools are then carried to the 1947 Whitin Model E spinning frame, where 96 roving ends are threaded onto the machine by hand. This machine twists the roving, turning it into yarn. The thickness of the yarn is regulated in several ways. The carding machine can be adjusted to make thicker or thinner roving; the spinning frame allows control over the drafting tension, the twist, and the number of strands that will be spun together for a particular yarn. Depending on the size of the lot it may take anywhere from a few hours to several days to spin. Bobbins of freshly spun yarn are placed in the steam box for 2–3 hours to set the twist.

After the steaming process is complete, Gail threads some types of yarns on the plying machine, another 1940s-era Whitin frame, adapted to fit our small space. This machine twists multiple strands of yarn in the opposite direction from their original spin. Varying the number of plies in a yarn provides an additional way to control its strength and thickness. The Spinnery's own plied yarns are mostly 2-ply, but we also produce 3- and 4-ply yarns.

Steamed and plied yarns then go to the finishing department, where they are skeined or coned.

9

CREATING COLORED YARNS

The Spinnery achieves a variety of colored yarns in several different ways. For our natural colored yarns, David sorts the raw fleece by its hue. The range of tones is wide, from white through grey and brown to black. Using blends of these natural fibers with dyed-in-the-wool colored fibers in different proportions yields various colors and gives the yarn a distinctive "tweedy" look. Mountain Mohair, Sylvan Spirit, and all the *GREENSPUN* and Organic yarns are mixed this way.

Cotton Comfort and Wonderfully Woolly are dyed as finished yarn. Since cotton and wool take up the dyes at different intensities, Cotton Comfort still has a flecked appearance. The Wonderfully Woolly line is a example of how dying different shades of base yarns can produce different results. Natural white, medium grey, and ragg yarns immersed in the same dye bath yield three distinctive colors. The Spinnery's fleece and yarns are not dyed in Putney but are sent to several small dye houses that specialize in low-impact dyeing.

Spinnery Sock Art is dyed by hand in very small batches by local artisan Melissa Johnson. The variegated and semisolid colors are dyed using nontoxic acid dyes. Each batch is usually 4–6 skeins, small amounts that allow for experimentation and variation, adding to the unique quality of the finished project.

The skeining machine winds off 12 skeins at a time. An automatic counter is set to turn it off when the desired number of yards has been wound. The ends of each skein are tied together and a safety tie is added for good measure.

Some of the Spinnery's yarns are washed after skeining to enhance their natural softness. Skeins are then weighed, twisted, and labeled by hand. Although these finishing steps are labor intensive, they allow us to see and feel each skein, serving as a final quality-control check. Yarns that do not meet our stringent standards are sold at a discount.

In addition to processing fiber into yarn, our staff also answers the phone, packs and invoices orders, and handles customer support. Many of us serve as sales clerks in the shop, and you're likely to find any one of us giving mill tours on specified days.

Not all our hours are spent making and selling yarn. Weekly staff meetings provide a forum for cooperative management; teams of owners and staff work together on marketing, finance, personnel, and new product development. And although the mill closes for the day at 5:30, there is often someone working late to get ready for the next day's production or to pack just one more order.

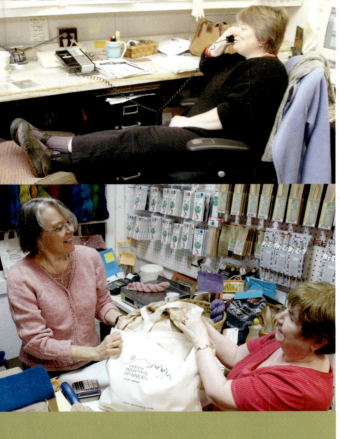

Our Knitting Patterns

Our knitting patterns are designed to celebrate the special characteristics of our yarns and to satisfy a variety of tastes. Because we want the time and effort that goes into any hand-knit project to be worthwhile, we design garments and accessories that will stand the test of time. We gravitate toward classic designs but enjoy adding modern twists and elegant techniques.

The patterns presented here were created by a dedicated team that includes co-op members Maureen Clark, Eric Robinson, and Margaret Atkinson, joined by staff Cap Sease and Melissa Johnson. Several of the patterns have been previously published individually. We are grateful to those of you who have contacted us with questions and comments; your experiences have helped us revise and refine them.

This collection ranges from easy to challenging; regardless of your knitting skills, you'll find projects to please. However, this is not a how-to book; we assume you know how to cast on, knit and purl (in the round and on straight needles), and bind off. You should also understand the conventions of written patterns and know how to produce and use a gauge swatch. There are many excellent basic books for knitters as well as wonderful online resources; we have listed some of our favorites in the Resources section at the end of this book.

KNIT A GAUGE SWATCH

We recommend that you start each project by knitting a gauge swatch, the best way to ensure that your garment will fit. A swatch also allows you to practice new stitches or techniques.

If the fabric is textured, make a practice cable or two. If it is Fair Isle, knit the chart and make sure you like your color choices. If your project is knit in the round, knit the swatch in the round. Most knitters knit and purl at different tensions, so a swatch knit flat may not give an accurate version of your fabric when created in the round. Once your swatch is complete, it is a good idea to gently wash it the way you would a finished garment. This will give the best preview of what your knitted fabric will be like.

This preliminary work will pay off, as you will be less likely to have to backtrack and the rhythm of the project will move forward more quickly, resulting in a more enjoyable and satisfying knitting experience and a well-fitting garment.

SIZING AND SCHEMATICS

The measurements presented in each pattern are for the finished garments. The schematics offer guidelines to the various parts of the garment, showing the basic shape and measurement of each piece.

There are several good ways to get measurements for a proper fit. We recommend measuring a sweater that fits you well. You will need a chest measurement, length from underarm to hem, sleeve length, and armhole depth. Your finished sweater should fit around the chest with 3- to 6-inch (8- to 16-cm) ease, depending on the garment's style. Choose your pattern size according to the finished chest measurement.

Sleeve length varies greatly from person to person. The same sweater size may fit two different people well in the body, but the sleeves may be too long or too short. To measure for the correct sleeve length, run a tape measure from the prominent bone on the back of the neck over a slightly bent elbow to the desired cuff. Then subtract ¼ of *the sweater's* chest measurement to get the appropriate sleeve length.

CUSTOM SPINNING FOR FARMERS & ARTISANS

From the beginning we have processed fiber sent from farms around the country, guaranteeing to each that the same fiber they send us for processing will be returned as a high-quality yarn or roving. David, our fleece grader and production manager, and Patty, our master spinner, work closely with farmers to develop yarns that use their particular types of fiber to best advantage.

Custom-processed yarns retain the character of the flock from which they came, so farmers can place a premium price on their local products. Production weavers and specialty blanket manufacturers have turned to the Spinnery as a regular source for yarns designed to meet their technical specifications.

Our custom processing business has grown to more than 60 percent of yearly production. Most of this custom work comes from farms in the Northeast. It is a major way we support our region's agriculture.

Annual fiber festivals such as those in Maryland and New Hampshire in the spring, and in Vermont and New York in the fall, are prime showcases for independent fiber producers and their custom-spun yarns. We enjoy seeing how the natural grey or white yarns spun in our mill are transformed by these creative artisans.

ABBREVIATIONS

[ ]	work instructions within brackets as many times as directed, or for entire row
( )	work instructions within parentheses in the place directed
CC	contrasting color
cm	centimeter
cn	cable needle
dec	decrease(s), decreasing
DK	double-knitting weight
dpn	double pointed needle(s)
g	gram(s)
h-bar(k)	insert right needle from front to back under the horizontal bar of previous row that extends between the needles and knit a st. *NB: This creates a hole, unlike m1, which twists the stitch.*
h-bar(p)	insert right needle from back to front under the horizontal bar of previous row that extends between the needles and purl a st. *NB: This creates a hole, unlike m1, which twists the stitch.*
inc	increase(s), increasing
k	knit
k1b	knit into back of st
kfb	knit into the front and back of st (increase)
k2tog	knit 2 sts together (right-leaning decrease)
L	large
MC	main color
M	medium
m	meter(s)
m1	make one increase—insert left needle from back to front under the bar between the st just worked and the next st and k this strand through the front
mm	millimeter(s)
NB	nota bene (take note)
oz	ounce(s)
p	purl
p2tog	purl 2 sts together
pm	place marker
psso	pass slipped st over
RS	right side
sc	single crochet
sl	slip
sm	slip marker
S	small
sl1, k1, psso	slip 1 st, k1 st, pass the slipped stitch over (left-leaning decrease)
sl1, k2tog, psso	slip 1 st, k2 sts tog, pass the slipped stitch over (double decrease)
ssk	slip 2 sts, one at a time, as if to knit; insert left needle into front of sts and knit tog (left-leaning decrease)
ssp	slip 2 sts, one at a time, as if to knit; replace together on left needle and purl tog through the back loops (left-leaning decrease)
st st	stockinette stitch
st, sts	stitch, stitches
tog	together
tbl	through back loop
W&T	wrap and turn: leaving working yarn where it is, slip next st purlwise, bring yarn between needles (to front or back), slip st back to left needle. Turn work and move yarn to working position.
WS	wrong side
wyib	with yarn in back
wyif	with yarn in front
XL	extra-large
yds	yard(s)
yo	yarn over

TECHNIQUES

Backward Loop Cast On *(also known as single cast on)*

Make a slipknot on the right needle. *Make a loop with the working yarn and place it on the needle so it doesn't unwind; repeat from *. *NB: There are many good videos online that demonstrate this simple cast on.*

Knit Cast On

Make a slipknot on the left needle. *Knit this st, leaving it on the needle, and slip the new st to the left needle. Repeat from *.

Cable Cast On *(in the middle of a project)*

Turn work. *Insert right-hand needle between the first two sts on left needle and wrap the yarn as if to knit. Place the new st on left needle; repeat from *.

Kitchener Stitch

Hold your needles parallel to each other with points in the same direction and yarn at the right end of back needle. Using a tapestry needle, weave together the two pieces as follows:

Set up: Pass the yarn through the first st on the front needle purlwise and then through the first st of the back needle knitwise. Pull yarn through, but do not pull it tight.

1: Pass the yarn through first stitch of front needle as if to knit and slip stitch off needle.

2: Pass yarn through next stitch on front needle as if to purl; leave stitch on needle and pull yarn through.

3: Pass yarn through first stitch on back needle as if to purl; slip stitch off needle.

4: Pass yarn through next stitch on back needle as if to knit; leave stitch on needle and pull yarn firm.

Repeat steps 1–4 until no more stitches remain. Pull yarn through to inside and fasten off.

Three-Needle Bind Off

Turn work inside out. Using two straight needles of any size, place sts for one back shoulder on one needle and sts for the corresponding front shoulder on the second needle, with needles pointing to the right. Hold these two needles together. With a third needle, knit into the first st on the front needle and the first st on back needle. Knit these two sts together. Repeat and pass the first st over the second st. Keeping tension fairly loose, continue to bind off in this manner. Break the yarn and pull it through the last st.

I-Cord *(over 3–6 sts)*

Place all sts on one dpn. *Knit one row. Without turning the work, slide sts to beginning of row. Pull yarn firmly from end of row. Repeat from *. Work in this manner until I-cord is desired length.

Tassel

Cut a piece of stiff cardboard approximately 3½ x 5 in (9 x 13 cm). Wrap yarn around shorter side until the tassel is as thick as you'd like it. Thread a doubled strand, about 9 in (23 cm), under all strands at one edge and tie in a secure knot. Cut the strands of the tassel at the opposite edge. Remove from cardboard and tie an additional strand below the top to make the "ball" of the tassel.

> *"When I first moved to Vermont, Green Mountain Spinnery introduced me to high-quality yarns. When offered the oppor-tunity to fill in for vacationing employees, I quickly grabbed the chance to make myself indispensable, guaranteeing my future with the company. Although I knew my knitting and computer skills were valuable assets, I never expected that I would also become a designer and tech editor."*
>
> ERIC

The Patterns

15

East Putney Aran

Designed by Melissa Johnson

An ideal first Aran, this sweater features an elegantly crafted V-neck and two simple yet striking cable motifs framed by seed stitch. Shown in Natural White New Mexico Organic.

SIZES: S/2–4 (M/6–8, L/10–12)

FINISHED MEASUREMENTS

CHEST: 26 (30, 34) in/66.5 (76.5, 86.5) cm
LENGTH TO UNDERARM: 9 (10, 11) in/23 (25.5, 28) cm
SLEEVE LENGTH TO UNDERARM: 11 (14, 16) in/28 (36, 41) cm

GAUGE: 26 sts and 32 rows in pattern over 4 in/10 cm

MATERIALS

YARN: 4 (5, 6) skeins of New Mexico Organic, Cotton Comfort, Sylvan Spirit, or Alpaca Elegance
NEEDLES: size 4 US/3.5 mm straight or circular needles, 24 in/60 cm long AND size 4 US/3.5 mm circular needle, 16 in/40 cm long

TERMS USED

kfb = increase by knitting into the front and back of st
pk = purl and knit into the next st
sl 1, p1, psso = slip one st purlwise, p1, pass slipped st over

For washing instructions read "Caring for Handknits" on page 114.

BODY

Back: Cast on 86 (98, 112) sts. Knit 1 (2, 1) Selvedge sts, work Chart 1 for your size, Chart 2, Chart 3 for your size, k1 (2, 1) selvedge sts. *NB: selvedge sts are knit on RS and purl on WS.* Work charts until Back measures 9 (10, 11) in / 23 (25.5, 28) cm, or desired length to underarm. Bind off 6 (8, 10) sts at the beginning of the next 2 rows. Continue in pattern as established until Back measures 14½ (16½, 18½) in / 37 (42, 47) cm. Place sts on holder or spare needle.

Front: Work as for Back to underarm. Bind off 6 (8, 10) sts at the beginning of the next 2 rows.

Shape Neck: On the following RS row, work 32 (36, 41) sts in pattern; then k2tog, p1, k1, kfb. Join a second ball of yarn and pk, k1, p1, ssk, work in pattern to end. *The neckband will be picked up over the two increased sts on either side of the neck, leaving two knit sts to outline the V.* Work WS row as established. On next RS row, work 31 (35, 40) sts in pattern, k2tog, p1, k2, kfb. *P1* With second ball of yarn, ~~pk~~ *P1*, k1, p1, ssk, work in pattern to end. Continue to decrease in this manner until 16 (17, 19) sts remain for each shoulder. Work straight until armhole measures 5½ (6½, 7½) in / 14 (16.5, 19) cm.

Join shoulders using three-needle bind off (see Techniques).

Leave remaining 42 (48, 54) sts on needle for back of neck.

Neckband: With 16 in / 40 cm circular needle and RS facing, begin at left shoulder seam; pick up and k32 (38, 44) sts along left neck edge, pm

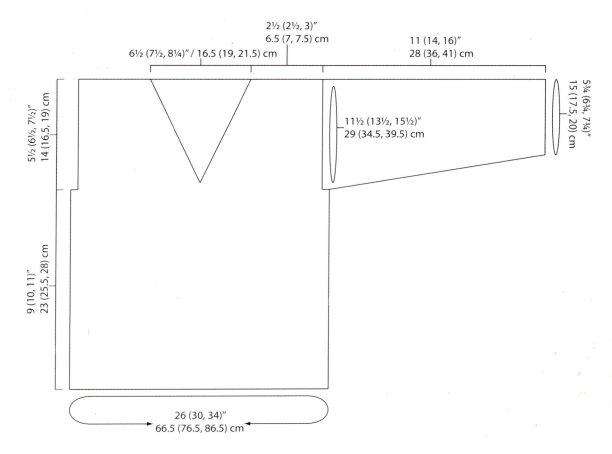

(place marker) for center front, pick up and k33 (39, 45) sts along right neck edge. *(This is approximately 3 sts for every 4 rows.)* Work across 42 (48, 54) sts for back neck. Work neckband in seed st as follows:

Round 1: pm, [p1, k1] to 2 sts before center front marker, p2tog, sl 1, p1, psso, [k1, p1] to end.

Round 2: [K1, p1] to 2 sts before center front marker, p2tog, sl 1, p1, psso, [p1, k1] to end.

Repeat Rounds 1 & 2, then bind off in seed st, working center decreases as before.

SLEEVES *(make 2)*

Cast on 38 (44, 50) sts. K1 selvedge st, begin pattern at point indicated on chart. Work across chart, end k1 selvedge st. Increase 1 st after first (selvedge) st and before last st every 4th row 12 (14, 14) times, then every 6th row 6 (8, 11) times—74 (86, 100) sts. *NB: Incorporate added sts into pattern, but wait until there are 4 sts before making a cable.* Work straight until sleeve measures 11 (14, 16) in / (28, 36, 41) cm. Bind off.

FINISHING

Sew sleeve and armhole seams. Weave in loose ends on wrong side of work.

KEY

☐ k on RS, p on WS

⊡ p on RS, k on WS

 slip 2 sts onto cn and hold in back, k2, k2 from cn

slip 2 sts onto cn and hold in front, k2, k2 from cn

Chart 3 - Small

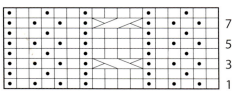

7
5
3
1

Chart 1 - Small

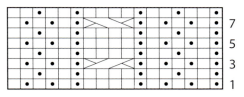

7
5
3
1

Chart 3 - Large

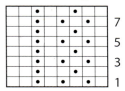

7
5
3
1

Medium size
uses only Chart 2

Chart 1 - Large

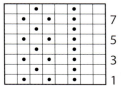

7
5
3
1

Chart 2 (body and sleeve)

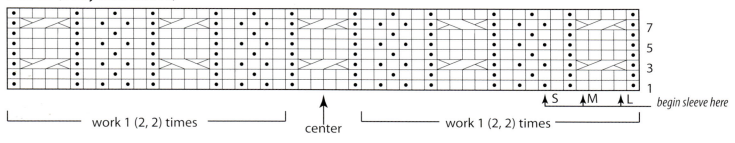

7
5
3
1

S   M   L   *begin sleeve here*

└─── work 1 (2, 2) times ───┘   center   └─── work 1 (2, 2) times ───┘

Ascutney Mountain Hat & Earwarmer

Designed by Melissa Johnson

The prototype for this pattern became a staff favorite on ski trips. This warm and flattering hat has a cabled band that is knit sideways and an attractive double decrease at the crown. The cabled band can be knit alone to wear as an earwarmer. Shown in Pumpkin Wonderfully Woolly.

SIZE: One size fits most

FINISHED MEASUREMENTS

CIRCUMFERENCE: 21 in / 53.5 cm

GAUGE: 18 sts and 28 rows in stockinette st, over 4 in / 10 cm. *NB: The row gauge is important for correct fit. Adjust needle size if necessary.*

MATERIALS

YARN: 2 skeins of Mountain Mohair or Green Mountain Green OR 1 skein of Wonderfully Woolly or Vermont or Maine Organic

NEEDLES: size 7 US / 4.5 mm circular needle, 16 in / 40 cm long
dpn, size 7 US / 4.5 mm
medium-size crochet hook

Provisional cast on: Using waste yarn, crochet a chain of 30 sts. Then, with circular needle and project yarn, pick up and knit 28 sts into back loops of chain.

HAT BAND

NB: First row of chart is a WS row. Working back and forth, follow chart, slipping the first and last sts of every right side row. When 16 repeats of the chart have been completed, join band together using three-needle bind off or Kitchener stitch (see Techniques).

HAT BAND LINING

With wrong side of work facing, pick up 1 st in each edge st (66 sts). Turn work so right side is facing, place marker and knit 1 round. In the next round, increase as follows: *[k2, m1] 10 times, k2*. Repeat from * to * twice more (96 sts). Knit for 3 in / 7.5 cm. Wrap and turn—with yarn in back, slip 1 st as if to purl, move yarn between needles to front of work, and move slipped st back to left needle. Turn work.

HAT CROWN

(You will now be working on what feels like the wrong side. When you fold the band up, the smooth side of stockinette will line the band and then switch to the outside above the band for the crown.) Knit on this side for 3 in / 7.5 cm.

Pattern Chart

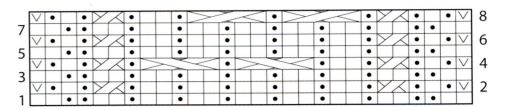

KEY

- ⊻ slip stitch
- ☐ k on RS, p on WS
- ⊡ p on RS, k on WS
- ⧄ slip first st to cn and hold at back; k1; k1 from cn
- ⧅ sl first 3 sts to cn and hold at back; k2; sl the p st from cn back onto left needle and p it; k2 from cn
- ⧅ sl first 3 sts to cn and hold at front; k2; sl the p st from cn back onto left needle and p it; k2 from cn

SHAPE CROWN

Change to dpn when necessary.
Round 1: *ssk, k12, k2tog; repeat from *.
Rounds 2, 4, 6, 8, 10, 12: knit.
Round 3: *ssk, k10, k2tog; repeat from *.
Round 5: *ssk, k8, k2tog; repeat from *.
Round 7: *ssk, k6, k2tog; repeat from *.
Round 9: *ssk, k4, k2tog; repeat from *.
Round 11: *ssk, k2, k2tog; repeat from *.
Round 13: *ssk, k2tog; repeat from *.
Round 14: k2tog around.

FINISHING

Break yarn, leaving 8 in / 20 cm. Using a tapestry needle, thread yarn through remaining sts and pull together firmly. Weave in loose ends on wrong side of work.

For washing instructions read "Caring for Handknits" on page 114.

Playful Sweaters for Children

Designer Melissa Johnson indulges her love of color and whimsical motifs in this collection of playful sweaters for all children. Knit in the round, each sweater features basic drop-shoulder construction, corrugated ribbing, and a choice of border design—flowers, diamonds, butterflies, cars, trucks, or sailboats. Shown in Cotton Comfort.

SIZES S/12–18 months (M/2–4 years, L/5–6 years)

FINISHED MEASUREMENTS

CHEST: Flowers, Diamonds, and Butterflies—20½ (25½, 30½) in/52 (65, 77.5) cm
Cars, Trucks, and Sailboats—23 (26, 29½) in/58.5 (66, 75) cm

LENGTH TO UNDERARM: 9½ (10, 10½) in/24.5 (25.5, 27) cm

GAUGE: 22 sts over 4 in/10 cm, using larger needle. For accuracy, check gauge over at least 4 in/10 cm in both solid and 2-color knitting. *NB: It may be necessary to change to smaller needles to maintain gauge in solid color knitting.*

MATERIALS

YARN: 3 (4, 5) skeins Main Color (MC), 1 skein each of colors A, B, C in Cotton Comfort
NEEDLES: size 4 US/3.5 mm AND size 5 US/3.75 mm circular needles, 24 in/60 cm long
dpn, size 4 US/3.5 mm AND size 5 US/3.75 mm
OPTIONAL: Size 4 US/3.5 mm circular needle, 16 in/40 cm long for neck
BUTTONS FOR WHEELS ON TRUCKS SWEATER: 14 (16, 18), approximately ½ in/1 cm

21

OUR COLORWAYS:

	Flowers	Diamonds	Butterflies
MC	Weathered Green	Violet	Unbleached White
Color A	Peony	Weathered Green	Bluet
Color B	Yarrow	Yarrow	Pink Lilac
Color C	Unbleached White	Unbleached White	Mint

	Trucks	Cars	Sailboats
MC	Silver	Yarrow	Denim
Color A	Storm	Denim	Violet
Color B	Violet	Violet	Yarrow
Color C	Weathered Green	Peony	Unbleached White

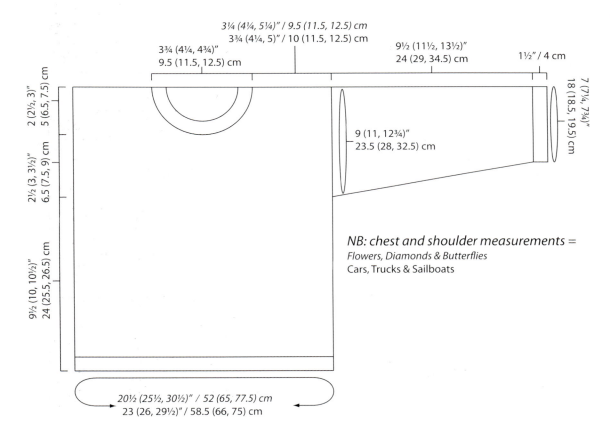

3¼ (4¼, 5¼)" / 9.5 (11.5, 12.5) cm
3¾ (4¼, 5)" / 10 (11.5, 12.5) cm

3¾ (4¼, 4¾)"
9.5 (11.5, 12.5) cm

9½ (11½, 13½)"
24 (29, 34.5) cm

1½" / 4 cm

7 (7¼, 7¾)"
18 (18.5, 19.5) cm

9 (11, 12¾)"
23.5 (28, 32.5) cm

2 (2½, 3)"
5 (6.5, 7.5) cm

2½ (3, 3½)"
6.5 (7.5, 9) cm

9½ (10, 10½)"
24 (25.5, 26.5) cm

NB: chest and shoulder measurements =
Flowers, Diamonds & Butterflies
Cars, Trucks & Sailboats

20½ (25½, 30½)" / 52 (65, 77.5) cm
23 (26, 29½)" / 58.5 (66, 75) cm

BODY

Flowers, Diamonds, and Butterflies: With smaller circular needle and MC, cast on 112 (140, 168) sts.

Cars, Trucks, and Sailboats: With smaller circular needle and MC, cast on 126 (144, 162) sts.

All sweaters: Place marker for beginning of round and join work, being careful not to twist

KEY

- ☐ mc
- ☒ color A
- ◉ color B
- ▨ color C
- • purl these stitches

Ribbing Chart

FLOWERS - 14 st repeat

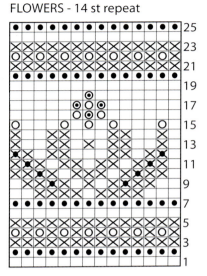

DIAMONDS - 14 st repeat

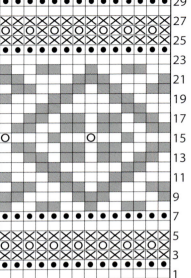

BUTTERFLIES - 14 st repeat

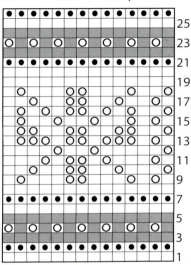

TRUCKS - 18 st repeat

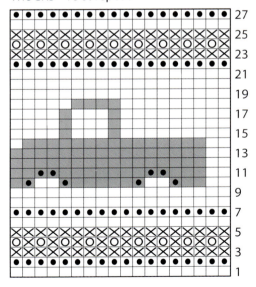

CARS - 18 st repeat

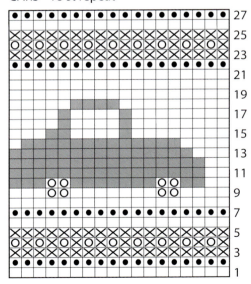

SAILBOATS - 18 st repeat

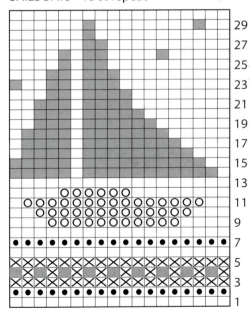

sts. Work Ribbing Chart. Change to larger needle and work Pattern Chart. After completing chart, knit with MC until sweater measures 9½ (10, 10½) in / 24 (25.5, 26.5) cm, or desired length to underarm. *NB: Change back to smaller needles if needed to maintain gauge.*

Divide for Armholes
Flowers, Diamonds, and Butterflies: knit 56 (70, 84) sts and place on holder for Front.
Cars, Trucks, and Sailboats: knit 63 (72, 81) sts and place on holder for Front.

BACK
All sweaters: Work remaining sts back and forth in stockinette stitch until Back measures 4½ (5½, 6½) in / 11.5 (14, 16.5) cm above beginning of armhole. Place sts on holder or spare circular needle.

FRONT
Knit sts from holder. Work in stockinette st until Front measures 2½ (3, 3½) in / 6.5 (7.5, 9) cm above beginning of armhole, ending with a purl row.
Flowers, Diamonds, and Butterflies: knit 18 (23, 29) sts, place 20 (24, 26) sts on holder for neck; join second ball of yarn and knit remaining 18 (23, 29) sts.

Cars, Trucks, and Sailboats: knit 21 (24, 27) sts, place 21 (24, 27) sts on holder for neck; join second ball of yarn and knit remaining 21 (24, 27) sts.

All sweaters: Working both Fronts with separate balls of yarn, purl one row. On the following row (Left Front), k to within 2 sts of neck edge,

k2tog. On right front, ssk, k to end. Decrease in this way every RS row for a total of 4 (5, 6) times—14 (18, 23) sts remain on each shoulder for Flowers, Diamonds, and Butterflies, 17 (19, 21) sts for Cars, Trucks, and Sailboats. Work straight until Front measures the same as Back.

Join Shoulders using the three-needle bind off (see Techniques).

NECKBAND
With smaller dpn (or 16 in / 40 cm circular) and MC (RS facing), knit Back neck sts, pick up and k3 sts for every 4 rows along side neck edge, knit Front neck sts, pick up and k3 sts for every 4 rows along 2nd neck edge. Place marker for beginning of round. Purl one round, decreasing if necessary to achieve an even number of sts. Work Rounds 3–5 of Pattern Chart. Knit one round MC.

Cars, Trucks, and Sailboats: Continuing with MC, knit one round, decreasing 0 (4, 6) sts evenly. Purl one round. Work 3 rounds of twisted rib (k1b, p1b), knit 4 rounds. Bind off loosely.

Flowers, Diamonds, and Butterflies: Work Ribbing Chart, work one round ribbing with MC, then bind off loosely.

SLEEVES
With dpn and MC and beginning at bottom of armhole, pick up and knit 50 (60, 70) sts. Place marker at beginning of round. Decrease 1 st at each side of marker every 1 in / 2.5 cm for sizes S and M, every ½ in / 1 cm for size L 6 (10, 14) times—38 (40, 42) sts. AT THE SAME TIME, when sleeve measures 9½ (11½, 13½) in / 24 (29,

34.5) cm or 1½ in / 4 cm less than desired length, work first 7 rounds of Pattern Chart. Change to smaller needles and work Ribbing Chart upside down (beginning with Round 6). Work one round ribbing with MC, then bind off loosely.

FINISHING
Weave in loose ends on wrong side of work. Sew buttons onto Truck sweater for wheels.

For washing instructions read "Caring for Handknits" on page 114.

Pebble Yoke Sweater & Hat

Designer Cap Sease is a knitter and weaver who is fascinated by the structure of fabric. Here she has added a pebble texture to the yoke of a classic baby sweater and hat.

SIZES: S/3–6 months (M/1 year, L/2 years)

FINISHED MEASUREMENTS

CHEST: 18 (20, 24) in / 46 (51, 61) cm
LENGTH TO SHOULDER: 10 (11, 13¾) in / 25.5 (28, 35) cm
HAT CIRCUMFERENCE: 13¼ (16¾, 18¾) in / 33.5 (42.5, 47.5) cm

GAUGE: 20 sts over 4 in / 10 cm for sizes 3–6 months and 1 year (in Sylvan Spirit); 18 sts over 4 in / 10 cm for size 2 (in Mountain Mohair)

MATERIALS

YARN: *for sweater:* 2 skeins Sylvan Spirit for S and M 3 skeins Mountain Mohair for size L
   hat requires 1 additional skein
NEEDLES: *for sizes S and M*—size 5 US / 3.75 mm circular needle, 24 in / 60 cm long; dpn, size 5 US / 3.75 mm
   for size L—size 7 US / 4.5 mm circular needle, 24 in / 60 cm long; dpn, size 7 US/4.5 mm
NOTIONS: 1 small and 1 medium stitch holder, 3 buttons

TERMS USED

kfb = increase by knitting into the front and back of st.
h-bar(k) = insert right needle from front to back under the horizontal bar of previous row that extends between the needles and knit a st. *NB: This creates a hole, unlike m1, which twists the stitch.*
h-bar(p) = insert right needle from back to front under the horizontal bar of previous row that extends between the needles and purl a st. *NB: This creates a hole, unlike m1, which twists the stitch.*

NB: The number of sts is the same for the 1- and 2-year sizes. The differences in yarn and gauge result in different sweater sizes.

YOKE

Using circular needle, cast on 50 (54, 54) sts.
Working back and forth, k 2 rows.
Next row: k4, *p2tog, yo; repeat from *, ending p2tog, k4—49 (53, 53) sts.

First buttonhole:
Next row (RS): k to last 4 sts, k2tog, yo, k2.
Next row (WS): k4, p to last 4 sts, k4.

Work the Pebble Pattern as follows. *The number of stitches is crucial for the pattern stitch to work; be sure to count total sts where the number is indicated.*

Row 1: k4, *kfb, k1; repeat from *, ending kfb, k4—70 (76, 76) sts

Row 2: k4, p to last 4 sts, k4.

Row 3: k4, *k2tog; repeat from *, ending k4—39 (42, 42) sts

Row 4: k4, *k1, h-bar(k); repeat from *, ending k5—69 (75, 75) sts

Row 5: k4, *kfb, k2; repeat from *, ending kfb, k4—90 (98, 98) sts

Row 6: same as Row 2.

Row 7: same as Row 3—49 (53, 53) sts

Row 8: same as Row 4—89 (97, 97) sts

Row 9: k4, *kfb, k3; repeat from *, ending kfb, k4—110 (120, 120) sts

Row 10: same as Row 2.

Row 11: same as row 3—59 (64, 64) sts

Row 12: same as row 4—109 (119, 119) sts

Row 13: k4, *kfb, k4; repeat from *, ending kfb, k2tog, yo, k2 (buttonhole)—130 (142, 142) sts

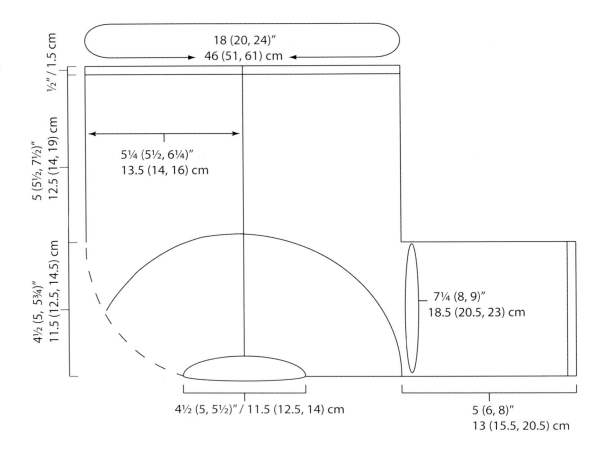

18 (20, 24)"
46 (51, 61) cm

½" / 1.5 cm

5 (5½, 7½)"
12.5 (14, 19) cm

5¼ (5½, 6¼)"
13.5 (14, 16) cm

4½ (5, 5¾)"
11.5 (12.5, 14.5) cm

7¼ (8, 9)"
18.5 (20.5, 23) cm

4½ (5, 5½)" / 11.5 (12.5, 14) cm

5 (6, 8)"
13 (15.5, 20.5) cm

Row 14: same as Row 2.

Row 15: same as Row 3—69 (75, 75) sts

Row 16: same as Row 4—129 (141, 141) sts

Row 17: k4 (5, 5), *kfb, k4; repeat from *, ending kfb, k4 (5, 5)—154 (168, 168) sts

Row 18: same as Row 2.

Row 19: same as Row 3—81 (88, 88) sts

Row 20: same as Row 4—153 (167, 167) sts

Row 21: k4 (6, 6), *kfb, k7 (6); repeat from *, ending kfb, k4 (6, 6)—172 (190, 190) sts

Row 22: same as Row 2.

Row 23: same as Row 3—90 (99, 99) sts

Row 24: same as Row 4—171 (189, 189) sts

Row 25: k85 (94, 94), kfb, k to end.

Row 26: same as Row 2.

Row 27: same as Row 3, ending k2tog, yo, k2 (buttonhole)—90 (99, 99) sts

Row 28: same as Row 4—171 (189, 189) sts

Row 29: k26 (28, 28) Left Front sts, pm (place marker), k36 (40, 40) Sleeve sts, pm, k47 (53, 53) Back sts, pm, k36 (40, 40) Sleeve sts, pm, k26 (28, 28) Right Front sts.

Keeping the first and last 4 sts in garter st, work in stockinette until the piece measures 4½ (5, 5¾) in / 11.5 (12.5, 14.5) cm, ending with a WS row. Break yarn, leaving a 4 in / 10 cm tail. With RS facing, place first 26 (28, 28) sts on a holder.

SLEEVES

Left Sleeve: Attach yarn and k the 36 (40, 40) left sleeve sts. Place remaining sts and markers on a holder or spare circular needle. Continue to work sleeve in st st until it measures 4½ (5½, 7½) in / 11.5 (14, 19) cm from underarm, or ½ in / 1.5 cm less than desired sleeve length, ending with a WS row. Finish the sleeve as follows:

Row 1: *k2tog; repeat from *.
Row 2: *k1, h-bar(k); repeat from *, ending k1.
Rows 3 & 4: knit.
Bind off.

Right Sleeve: Transfer the 36 (40, 40) Right Sleeve sts to needle and work as for Left Sleeve.

BODY

Return the 26 (28, 28) Right Front sts, 47 (53, 53) Back sts and 26 (28, 28) Left Front sts to needle—99 (109, 109) sts. Keeping the first and last 4 sts in garter st, work in stockinette until the piece measures 5 (5½, 7½) in / 12.5 (14, 19) cm from underarm, or ½ in / 1.5 cm less than desired length, ending with a WS row. Finish as follows:
Row 1: k4, *k2tog; repeat from *, ending k5.
Row 2: k4, *h-bar(k), k1; repeat from *, ending k5.
Rows 3 & 4: knit.
Bind off.

FINISHING

Sew sleeve seams. Sew on buttons. Weave in loose ends on wrong side of work.

NB: The number of sts is the same for the 1- and 2-year sizes. The differences in yarn and gauge result in different hat sizes.

Cast on 66 (84, 84) sts, using dpn. Divide evenly onto 3 needles. Join work, being careful not to twist sts. Work 8 rounds st st. Then begin pattern:

Round 1: *k2tog; repeat from *.
Round 2: *p1, h-bar(p); repeat from *. *Be sure to count sts after this round. It is easy to forget the last inc on each needle.*
Rounds 3 & 4: knit.

Work these 4 rounds 7 (8, 8) more times, ending with Round 2.

Decrease:
1st Decrease Round: *k1, k2tog; repeat from *—44 (56, 56) sts
Work Pattern Rounds 4, 1, & 2.
2nd Decrease Round: *k2, k2tog; repeat from *, ending k4 (0, 0)—34 (42, 42) sts
Work Pattern Rounds 4, 1, & 2.
3rd Decrease Round: *k2, k2tog; repeat from *, ending k2—26 (32, 32) sts
Work Pattern Rounds 4, 1, & 2.
4th Decrease Round: *k2tog; repeat from *—13 (16, 16) sts
Round 4: knit.
5th Decrease Round: *k2tog; repeat from *, ending k1 (0, 0)—7 (8, 8) sts

I-CORD

Place all 7 (8, 8) sts on 1 needle and work I-cord for desired length (see Techniques). Break yarn, leaving about 5 in / 12.5 cm. Using a tapestry needle, thread yarn through remaining sts and pull together firmly. Weave in loose ends on wrong side of work.

For washing instructions read "Caring for Handknits" on page 114.

Child's Striped Raglan

An old favorite revived, this top-down raglan sweater can be made with a crew neck or a placket. This is the type of sweater youngsters live in. Shown in Mountain Mohair (Coral Bell and Edelweiss). Also shown in Wonderfully Woolly (Black Walnut and Pumpkin) on page 19.

SIZES: 2 (4, 6, 8, 10)

FINISHED MEASUREMENTS

CHEST: 24 (26¾, 29¼, 31, 33¾) in /61 (67.5, 74.5, 79, 86) cm

LENGTH TO UNDERARM: 8 (8½, 9, 10, 11) in /20 (21.5, 23, 25.5, 28) cm

SLEEVE LENGTH TO UNDERARM: 9 (9½, 10, 10½, 11½) in /23 (24, 25.5, 26.5, 29) cm

GAUGE: 18 sts and 26 rows over 4 in /10 cm on larger needles

MATERIALS

YARN: 3 (4, 4, 4, 5) skeins Main Color (MC) and 1 skein Contrasting Color (CC) in Mountain Mohair OR 2 (2, 2, 3, 3) skeins Main Color (MC) and 1 skein Contrasting Color (CC) in Wonderfully Woolly or Vermont or Maine Organic

NEEDLES: size 5 US /3.75 mm AND size 7 US /4.5 mm circular needles, 16 in /40 cm long AND 24 in /60 cm long for larger sizes
dpn size 5 US /3.75 mm AND size 7 US /4.5 mm

NOTIONS: 2 stitch holders, 4 markers

TERMS USED

kfb = increase by knitting into the front and back of st

m1 = insert left needle from back to front under the bar between the st just worked and the next st and k this strand through the front

The back neck is worked back and forth in short rows, to lower the front neck line.

BODY (*Directions are for either a placket or crew neck*)
Using MC and larger circular needle, cast on 36 (38, 40, 42, 42) sts. Do not join.

Rows 1, 3, 5, 7, 9 (WS): purl.
Row 2: k1, kfb, pm (place marker), kfb, k4, kfb, pm, kfb, k18 (20, 22, 24, 24), kfb, pm, kfb, k4, kfb, pm, kfb, k1.

With RS facing, the four markers now on the needle are markers 1, 2, 3, and 4. The sts between markers 1 and 2 will be the Left Sleeve sts; sts between markers 3 and 4 will be the Right Sleeve.

Row 4: k2, kfb, sm (slip marker), kfb, k6, kfb, sm, kfb, k20 (22, 24, 26, 26), kfb, sm, kfb, k6, kfb, sm, kfb, k2.
Row 6: *k to 1 st before marker, kfb, sm, kfb, repeat from * 3 times, k to end.
Rows 8 and 10: k2, m1, *k to 1 st before marker, kfb, sm, kfb, repeat from * 3 times, k to last 2 sts, m1, k2.

Placket version: *The stripe pattern can be started as the placket is being worked or after the placket is complete.*
Row 11: purl; cast on 6 (7, 8, 9, 9) sts at end of row.
Row 12: Repeat Row 6; cast on 6 (7, 8, 9, 9) sts at end of row.
Row 13: k3, purl to last 3 sts, k3.
Row 14: Repeat Row 6.

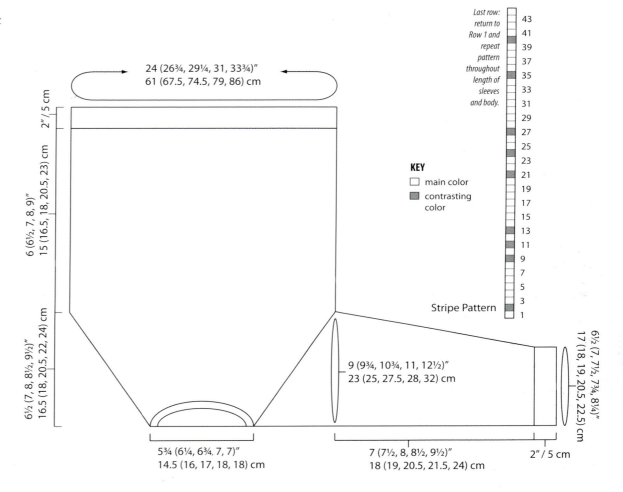

Last row: return to Row 1 and repeat pattern throughout length of sleeves and body.

43
41
39
37
35
33
31
29
27
25
23
21
19
17
15
13
11
9
7
5
3
1

KEY
☐ main color
▧ contrasting color

Stripe Pattern

24 (26¾, 29¼, 31, 33¾)"
61 (67.5, 74.5, 79, 86) cm

2" / 5 cm

6 (6½, 7, 8, 9)"
15 (16.5, 18, 20.5, 23) cm

6½ (7, 8, 8½, 9½)"
16.5 (18, 20.5, 22, 24) cm

5¾ (6¼, 6¾, 7, 7)"
14.5 (16, 17, 18, 18) cm

9 (9¾, 10¾, 11, 12½)"
23 (25, 27.5, 28, 32) cm

7 (7½, 8, 8½, 9½)"
18 (19, 20.5, 21.5, 24) cm

6½ (7, 7½, 7¾, 8¼)"
17 (18, 19, 20.5, 22.5) cm

2" / 5 cm

Work the last two rows 3 (3, 4, 5, 5) more time—132 (136, 148, 160, 160) sts.

Crew Neck version:
Row 11: purl.
Row 12: Repeat Row 6; cast on 12 (14, 16, 18, 18) sts at end of row.

Placket or Crew Neck:
Join sts and begin working in the round, knitting all sts and making increases before and after each marker every other round. Work Stripe Pattern, changing colors at marker 2. Change to longer needle when necessary. Work until there are 40 (44, 48, 50, 56) sts for Sleeves and 54 (60, 66, 70, 76) sts for Front and Back.

Divide work:
Work to marker 1, place sleeve sts on holder; work to marker 3, place sleeve sts on holder, work to end of round. Continue knitting 108 (120, 132, 140, 152) body sts, maintaining stripe

pattern and changing colors under left Sleeve, until Body measures 6 (6½, 7, 8, 9) in / 15 (16.5, 18, 20.5, 23) cm from underarm, or desired length. Change to smaller needle and work k1, p1 ribbing for 2 in / 5 cm. Bind off loosely.

SLEEVES *(make 2)*

Divide sts for one Sleeve onto larger dpn. Maintaining stripe pattern and changing colors at the underarm, work for 1 in / 2.5 cm. Then decrease as follows: beginning at underarm k1, k2tog, k to 3 sts from end of round, k2tog, k1. Repeat this decrease every 1 in / 2.5 cm 4 (5, 6, 6, 7) more times—30 (32, 34, 36, 40) sts. Work until Sleeve measures 7 (7½, 8, 8½, 9½) in / 18 (19, 20.5, 21.5, 23) cm from underarm, or desired length. Change to smaller needle and work k1, p1 ribbing for 2 in / 5 cm. Bind off loosely.

NECK BAND

Placket: Using smaller circular needle and with RS facing, pick up and k59 (63, 67, 71, 73) sts. Work k1, p1 ribbing for 4 rows. Bind off loosely.

Crew Neck: Using smaller dpn and with RS facing, begin at back left neck. Pick up and k59 (63, 67, 71, 73) sts. Work k1, p1 ribbing for 4 rounds. Bind off loosely.

FINISHING

Weave in loose ends on wrong side of work. Sew small holes at underarms.

For washing instructions read "Caring for Handknits" on page 114.

"After attending a New England Needle Arts show and seeing the GMS booth, I fell in love with the yarn. I started coming up to the Spinnery for knitters' weekends and enjoyed it so much, I knew this was where I was supposed to be! My house sold in a day, my husband's business sold in three, and we were off to Putney. I was working at the Spinnery the very next week. That was 11 years ago."
MAUREEN

Grandma's Delight Sweater & Hat

A delightful lace sweater for little ones, this pattern was revised for DK weight yarn from a design by Libby Mills. The hat, designed by Cap Sease, is the perfect topper to the sweater. A great project to learn the basics of lace knitting with.

SIZES: 0–6 (6–18, 18–30) months

FINISHED MEASUREMENTS

CHEST: 17½ (21½, 25½) in / 44.5 (54.5, 65) cm
HAT CIRCUMFERENCE: 13 (16, 18) in / 33 (40.5, 45.5) cm

GAUGE: 24 sts in pattern over 4 in / 10 cm

MATERIALS

YARN: 3 (4, 4) skeins Cotton Comfort, Sylvan Spirit, or New Mexico Organic
NEEDLES: Size 5 US / 3.75 mm circular needle, 24 in / 60 cm long
dpn, size 5 US / 3.75 mm
NOTIONS: small stitch holders, 6 (7, 8) buttons

For washing instructions read "Caring for Handknits" on page 114.

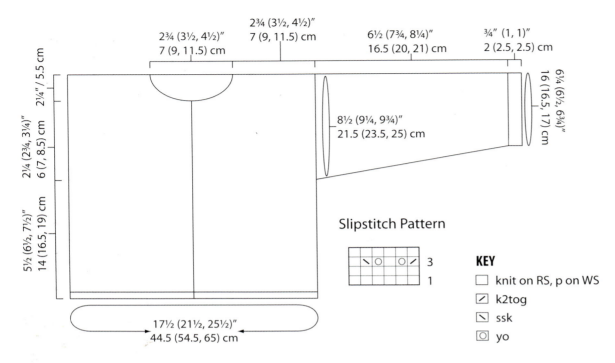

Slipstitch Pattern

	＼	○		○	／		3
							1

KEY

☐ knit on RS, p on WS

☑ k2tog

☒ ssk

⊙ yo

SWEATER INSTRUCTIONS

BODY

Cast on 111 (135, 159) sts. Work 4 rows ribbing:

Row 1: k1, *p1, k1; repeat from *.

Row 2: p1, *k1, p1; repeat from *.

Make buttonhole: k1, p1, k1, yo, ssk, p1, k1, continue in ribbing to end of row.

Work one more row of ribbing.

*NB: **Buttonholes** are placed at even intervals on the right front buttonhole band as the body is knit. If making a longer or shorter sweater, adjust the spacing of buttonholes accordingly.*

On next round, begin Slipstitch Pattern:

Right Front: work 7 sts in rib, 24 (30, 36) sts in pattern.

Back: k1 ("seam" st), work 48 (60, 72) sts in pattern.

Left Front: k1 ("seam" st), work 24 (30, 36) sts in pattern, 6 sts in rib.

Slipstitch Pattern:

Row 1: knit.

Rows 2 & 4: purl.

Row 3: *k2tog, yo, k1, yo, ssk, k1; repeat from *.

Continue ribbing and pattern, maintaining side "seam" sts in stockinette st and making buttonholes every 1½ (1½, 2) in / 4 (4, 5) cm. When body measures 5½ (6½, 7½) in / 14 (16.5, 19) cm from beginning, or desired length to underarm.

Divide for Fronts and Back:

Work across 31 (37, 43) Right Front sts; place on holder. Work across 49 (61, 73) Back sts; place on second holder. Cast on 1 st (this additional st will be used when sewing in the sleeve and is worked in stockinette). Work across remaining sts. There are 31 (37, 43) sts for Left Front.

Left Front: Continue until piece measures 2¼ (2¾, 3¼) in / 6 (7, 8.5) cm from beginning of armhole, ending on Row 1 or 3 of pattern. On next row, work first 11 (11, 14) sts and place on holder, work to end of row. Decrease at neck edge on the next 4 (6, 6) rows—17 (21, 24) sts. Continue in pattern until armhole measures approximately 4½ (5, 5½) in / 11.5 (12.5, 14) cm, ending on Row 4 of Slipstitch Pattern. Place sts on a holder.

Right Front: Transfer sts from holder to needle, join new ball of yarn at underarm, cast on 1 st and resume pattern, a WS row. Work as for Left Front, reversing shaping at neck edge. Continue until armhole measures same as Left Front; place sts on holder.

Back: Transfer sts from holder to needle; with new ball of yarn, cast on 1 st, work in pattern to end, cast on 1 st—51 (63, 75) sts. Work in pattern until armhole measures the same as fronts, ending on Row 4 of Slipstitch Pattern.

Join Shoulders: Turn body of sweater inside out and join shoulders using the three-needle bind off (see Techniques). Turn sweater right side out. There are 17 (21, 27) sts left for back of neck.

NECK RIBBING

Transfer 11 (11, 14) sts of Right Front to needle, pick up and knit 12 (16, 16) sts along right neck edge, transfer 17 (21, 27) sts from Back, pick up and knit 12 (16, 16) sts along left neck edge, transfer 11 (11, 14) sts of Left Front to needle. Work k1, p1 ribbing for 4 rows. Bind off loosely.

SLEEVES (make two)

Cast on 37 (39, 41) sts; work in k1, p1 ribbing for ¾ (1, 1) in / 2 (2.5, 2.5) cm. On next row, k1 (2, 3), work Pattern Stitch, end k0 (1, 2). Increase 1 st at each end of every 6th row 7 (8, 9) times, keeping added sts in stockinette until there are enough to incorporate new sts into pattern, leaving 1 st at each edge for seam—51 (55, 59) sts. Continue until sleeve measures 7¼ (8¾, 9¼) in / 18.5 (22.5, 23.5) cm from ribbing, ending with Row 4. Bind off.

FINISHING

Sew sleeve seams; sew sleeves in place. Weave in loose ends on wrong side of work. Sew on buttons.

HAT INSTRUCTIONS

Cast on 78 (96, 108) sts. Divide onto 3 needles, with each group of sts divisible by 6. Join work, being careful not to twist sts. Knit 4 rounds.

Begin Slipstitch Pattern:

Rounds 1, 2, & 3: knit.
Round 4: *k2tog, yo, k1, yo, ssk, k1; repeat from * to end.

Continue in this way until Slipstitch Pattern measures approximately 3½ (4½, 5½) in / 9 (11.5, 14) cm, ending with Round 1.

Decrease

Round 1: *k1, k2tog; repeat from *—52 (64, 72) sts
Round 2: knit.
Round 3: *k2, k2tog; repeat from *—39 (48, 54) sts
Round 4: knit.

From here on the decreases are different for different sizes.

0–6 months:

Round 5: k2, k2tog, *k1, k2tog, k2, k2tog; repeat from *—28 sts
Rounds 6 & 8: knit.
Round 7: *k1, k2tog; repeat from *, end k1—19 sts
Round 9: k1, *k2tog; repeat from *—10 sts

6–18 months:

Round 5: *k2, k2tog; repeat from *—36 sts
Rounds 6, 8, & 10: knit.
Round 7: *k1, k2tog; repeat from *—24 sts
Round 9: *k1, k2tog; repeat from *—16 sts
Round 11: *k2tog; repeat from *—8 sts

18–30 months:

Round 5: *k2, k2tog; repeat from *, end k2—41 sts
Rounds 6, 8, & 10: knit.
Round 7: *k1, k2tog; repeat from *, end k2—28 sts
Round 9: *k1, k2tog; repeat from *, end k1—19 sts
Round 11: k1, *k2tog; repeat from *—10 sts

FINISHING

All sizes: Finish with I-cord or pom-pom.

I-CORD

After decreases have been completed, k2tog around until 5 sts remain. Place all sts on 1 needle and work I-cord for desired length (see Techniques). Break yarn, leaving about 5 in / 12.5 cm. Using a tapestry needle, thread yarn through remaining sts and pull together firmly. Weave in loose ends on wrong side of work.

POM-POM

Break yarn, leaving about 6 in / 15 cm. Using a tapestry needle, thread yarn through remaining sts and pull together firmly. Make a pom-pom and attach securely to the center of crown. Weave in loose ends on wrong side of work.

Stripy Stripe Sweater

Designed by Cap Sease

There are many colorful ways to make this pullover as distinctive as the child who wears it. This worsted weight pattern uses contrasting colors to make a striking yoke. This is an excellent project to combine new yarns for the main color and "stash" yarns for the contrasting colors. This is also a great project to use with that special skein of hand-painted or handspun yarn. Shown in Wonderfully Woolly.

SIZES: S/4 (M/6, L/8, XL/10)

FINISHED MEASUREMENTS

CHEST: 26 (28, 30, 32) in/66 (71, 76, 81.5) cm
LENGTH TO UNDERARM: 8½ (9½, 10½, 11½) in/21.5 (24, 27, 29) cm

GAUGE: 18 sts in stockinette st, over 4 in/10 cm

MATERIALS

YARN: 2 (3, 3, 3) skeins Main Color (MC) and 1 skein Contrasting Color (CC) in Wonderfully Woolly or Vermont or Maine Organic
3 (4, 4, 5) skeins MC and 1 (1, 1, 2) skeins CC in Mountain Mohair
NEEDLES: size 6 US/4 mm circular needles, 16 in/40 cm AND 24 in/60 cm long
NOTIONS: 1 large stitch holder or spare circular needle

BODY

Back: Using MC and longer circular needle, cast on 58 (64, 68, 72) sts. Join CC and work in garter st (knit every row) for 4 rows—2 rows CC, 2 rows MC. Work in stockinette st in MC until piece measures 8½ (9½, 10½, 11½) in / 21.5 (24, 27, 29) cm or desired length to underarm, ending with a WS row. Work striped yoke in garter st as follows: 2 rows MC, 2 rows CC. Repeat these 4 rows until yoke measures 6½ (7, 7½, 8) in / 16.5 (18, 19, 20) cm. Knit 1 row MC and place stitches on holder.

Front: Work the same as for the Back until the striped yoke measures 3½ (4, 5½, 6) in / 9 (10, 14, 15) cm. With RS facing and maintaining the color sequence of stripes, k24 (26, 28, 29), bind off 10 (12, 12, 14) sts, knit to end. Working each side separately, k2tog at neck edge on next row and every RS row until there are 18 (20, 20, 22) sts for each shoulder. Work even until yoke measures the same as Back.

Join shoulders using the three-needle bind off (see Techniques). Place remaining 22 (24, 28, 28) Back sts on holder.

SLEEVES *(make 2)*

Left Sleeve: With RS facing and beginning at the bottom edge of the colored yoke on the left Front, use MC to pick up and k56 (64, 66, 70) sts (approximately 1 st for each valley between the purl ridges), ending at the bottom edge of the yoke on the left Back. Knit back. Work garter st—2 rows CC, 2 rows MC until there are 4 (4, 5, 7) color stripes, ending with 2 rows MC. Then work stockinette st in MC. AT THE SAME TIME, on the first k row of the second

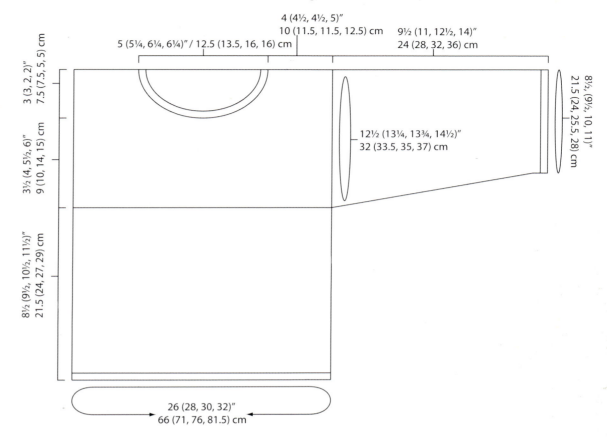

CC stripe, decrease 1 st at each end of the row. Decrease in the same way every following 8th row 5 (5, 9, 9) times, then every 4th row 3 (5, 0, 0) times—38 (42, 46, 50) sts. Work even until sleeve measures 9 (10½, 12, 13½) in / 22.5 (26.5, 30.5, 34.5) cm or ½ in / 1.5 cm less than desired length. Knit 2 rows MC, 2 rows CC, 1 row MC. Bind off.

Right Sleeve: Work same as Left Sleeve.

NECKBAND

Using shorter circular needle and MC, begin at the left side of the neck. Pick up and knit

approximately 16 (18, 16, 12) sts (approximately 1 st for each valley between the purl ridges) along the left side of neck, 12 (12, 13, 14) sts along the Front, approximately 16 (18, 16, 12) sts along the right side of neck and k22 (24, 28, 28) Back sts from the holder. There are approximately 66 (72, 73, 74) sts. Work 3 rows garter st, beginning with a p round. Bind off loosely.

FINISHING
Weave in loose ends on wrong side of work.

For washing instructions read "Caring for Handknits" on page 114.

On Your Toes Sweater

Designed by Eric Robinson

With its flattering diagonal ribs and a couture attention to detail, this V-neck cardigan is a joy to make and to wear. This pattern challenges ideas about the "right" way to do things, or at least puts a new twist on the tried and true with eyelets made without yarn-overs, decreases that feel like they're

pointing the wrong way, and set-in sleeves from the top down. Stay focused and read the directions carefully—the fun awaits. Shown in Charcoal Alpaca Elegance.

SIZES: S (M, L, XL)

FINISHED MEASUREMENTS

CHEST: 34 (37, 40, 42) in / 86.5 (94, 101.5, 106.5) cm
LENGTH TO UNDERARM: approximately 11 (12, 13, 13) in / 28 (30.5, 33, 33) cm

GAUGE: 22 sts and 32 rows over 4 in / 10 cm

MATERIALS

YARN: 7 (7, 8, 9) skeins of Sylvan Spirit or Alpaca Elegance
NEEDLES: size US 3 / 3.25 mm AND US 5 / 3.75 mm circular needles, 29 in / 80 cm long
size US 5 / 3.75 mm circular needle, 16 in / 40 cm long
dpn, size 5 US / 3.75 mm
NOTIONS: markers, stitch holders, small safety pins, 5 buttons, ½ in / 1.5 cm

TERMS USED

h-bar(k) (eyelet) = insert right needle from front to back under the horizontal bar of previous row that extends

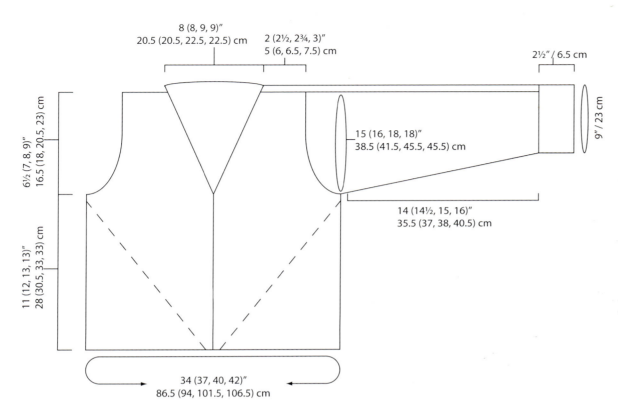

8 (8, 9, 9)"
20.5 (20.5, 22.5, 22.5) cm

2 (2½, 2¾, 3)"
5 (6, 6.5, 7.5) cm

2½" / 6.5 cm

9" / 23 cm

15 (16, 18, 18)"
38.5 (41.5, 45.5, 45.5) cm

6½ (7, 8, 9)"
16.5 (18, 20.5, 23) cm

14 (14½, 15, 16)"
35.5 (37, 38, 40.5) cm

11 (12, 13, 13)"
28 (30.5, 33, 33) cm

34 (37, 40, 42)"
86.5 (94, 101.5, 106.5) cm

between the needles and knit a st. *NB: This creates a hole, unlike m1, which twists the st.*

h-bar(p) (eyelet) = with yarn in front, insert right needle from back to front under the horizontal bar of previous row that extends between the needles and purl a st.

W & T = with yarn in back, sl next st as if to p. Bring yarn to front and return st to left needle. Turn work.

wyib = with yarn in back

wyif = with yarn in front

BODY *(Worked in one piece to the armholes):* Using larger 29 in / 80 cm needle, cast on 196 (212, 228, 244) sts.

First Set-up Row (RS): k3 (3, 3, 7) *[p2, k2] 11 (12, 13, 13) times, p2, k1, pm (place marker) for side "seam"; k1, [p2, k2] 11 (12, 13, 13) times*, p2, k0 (0, 0, 4), sl 1 wyib, pm (center back), sl 1, k0 (0, 0, 4). Repeat from * to * one time, end p2, k3 (3, 3, 7).

Second Set-up Row: slip first st wyif, *k the knits and p the purls to the last st before underarm marker, sl 1, sm (slip marker), sl 1*, work to center back. Repeat from * to *, work to end, sl last st.

Begin Receding Rib Pattern:

Row 1: *k to first p st, h-bar(k), p2. Then [k1, ssk, h-bar(p), p1] to 5 sts before marker; k1, ssk, p1, k1, sm, k1, p1, k2tog, k1; [p1, h-bar(p), k2tog, k1] to last p sts before center back marker, p2, h-bar(k)*, k to marker. Repeat from * to * (on repeat, work to last p sts before end of row, p2, h-bar(k), k to end).

Rows 2, 4, 6, 8: sl first st wyif, *k the knits and p the purls to the last st before underarm marker, sl 1, sm, sl 1*, work to center back, repeat from * to *, work to end, sl last st. *Make sure you slip all 6 designated sts on each WS row. These slipped sts will make a tiny float on the WS.*

Row 3: *k to first p st, h-bar(k), p2. Then [k1, ssk, h-bar(p), p1] to 4 sts before marker; k1, ssk, k1, sm, k1, k2tog, k1; [p1, h-bar(p), k2tog, k1] to last p sts before center back or end of row, p2, h-bar(k)*, k to marker. Repeat from * to *, k to end.

Row 5: *k to first p st, h-bar(k), p2. Then [k1, ssk, h-bar(p), p1] to 3 sts before marker; k1, k2tog, sm, ssk, k1, [p1, h-bar(p), k2tog, k1] to last p sts before center back or end of row, p2, h-bar(k)*, k to marker. Repeat from * to *, k to end. *NB: To prevent gaps, give a little extra tug to the consecutive k2tog and ssk at underarm "seams."*

Row 7: *k to first p st, h-bar(k), p2. Then [k1, ssk, h-bar(p), p1] to 2 sts before marker; k2tog, sm, ssk, [p1, h-bar(p), k2tog, k1] to last p sts before center back or end of row, p2, h-bar(k)*, k to marker. Repeat from * to *, k to end.

Repeat these 8 rows until the only ribbing left is at underarms. End with Row 7 when last knit rib st is "eaten" by the underarm rib, leaving only p2, k2, p2.

Dividing Row (WS): Work in pattern to 6 (6, 7, 8) sts before the last marker (center back marker may now be removed); place remaining 56 (60, 65, 70) sts on a holder for Right Front. Turn, work RS to 6 (6, 7, 8) sts before last marker. W & T; place remaining 56 (60, 65, 70) sts on a holder for Left Front.

Back: Rows 1 and 2: Work to 3 sts before holder. W & T, adding the 3 sts on left needle to holder.

Row 3: purl across, slipping first and last sts and placing a small safety pin to mark this row

(helpful later when measuring armhole).

Decrease Row: k1, k2tog, work to 3 sts from end, ssk, k1. Repeat Decrease Row every RS row 7 (9, 9, 10) more times—62 (66, 72, 76) sts. Work even until armhole measures 6½ (7, 8, 9) in / 16.5 (18, 20.5, 23) cm from marked row. Place sts on holders as follows: 10 (12, 13, 15) for Shoulder, 42, (42, 46, 46) for Neck, 10 (12, 13, 15) for Shoulder.

Left Front: Leaving 15 (15, 17, 19) sts on the holder at underarm, slip 44 (48, 51, 54) sts for Left Front onto needle ready to work RS. Join yarn and knit one row. Next row: sl 1, p40 (44, 47, 50), W & T. Add the 3 sts on left needle to holder. Work 2 rows even, reestablishing slipped sts at ends of WS rows. Dec at sleeve edge every other row, as follows: k1, k2tog, k to end. AT THE SAME TIME, on the 4th dec row, begin neck decreases: On RS, work sleeve dec, k to 3 sts from end, ssk, k1. Discontinue sleeve decs after 8 (10, 10, 11) have been completed; continue neck decs every other row for a total of 23 (23, 25, 25)—10 (12, 13, 15) sts. Work even until armhole measures the same as Back. Put sts on holder.

Right Front: Slip 56 (60, 65, 70) Right Front sts onto needle ready to work WS, leaving 3 sts on holder at underarm. Work 1 row, keeping underarm sts in pattern and slipping the last st. On next row, k44 (48, 51, 54), W & T. Add the 12 (12, 14, 16) remaining sts to holder. Work one row even. On next RS row, knit back to 3 sts before holder, W & T. Add the 3 sts on left needle to holder. Purl one row, slipping edge sts. Then dec at sleeve edge every other row as follows: knit to 3 sts from end, ssk, k1. Continue

shaping as for Left Front, decreasing with k2tog at neck edge and ssk at sleeve edge.

Join Shoulders:
You will knit a strip, beginning at the neck edge, and attaching to Front and Back as you go. Place shoulder sts from left Back on a dpn (needle #1). Place Left Front shoulder sts on dpn #2. On a 3rd needle, cast on 8 sts; these are the saddle sts. Using neck end of needle #2 and the sts on needle #3, work Row 1 (RS): sl 1 wyif, p2, k2, p2, sl 1 wyif. Turn. Put down needle #3. Position work so that the WS of Back shoulder is on your right and the WS of front shoulder is on your left with the saddle sts in the middle. Be careful not to twist the Front. *It may be helpful to lay out the work on a table to position it properly.* Row 2: With WS of Back shoulder facing and yarn in back, sl 1 st from needle #1 to #2, then, using the yarn strand from the saddle sts, ssk this st with first saddle st. K2, p2, k2, then k2tog (a st from Front shoulder with a saddle st). Repeat Rows 1 & 2 until all shoulder sts are connected to the saddle. Place remaining 8 sts on a safety pin. Repeat for right shoulder, placing Front sts on needle #1 and Back sts on #2. After Row 1, position work so that the WS of Back shoulder is on your left and the WS of Front shoulder is on your right with the saddle sts in the middle. Then proceed with Row 2.

SLEEVES *(make 2)*
With RS facing, measure 2¼ (2¼, 2½, 3) in / 5.5 (5.5, 6.5, 7.5) cm from shoulder center along armhole edge to each side. Mark these points with small safety pins. The section between these pins, including the shoulder sts, is part A. Place 2 more pins 4 (4½, 4½, 5½) in / 10 (11.5,

11.5, 14) cm from first pins. These are parts B. The final section, which includes the underarm sts, is part C.

Part A: With RS facing and shorter circular needle, pick up and k6 (6, 7, 8) sts between pin on Left Front for left Sleeve and on Back for right Sleeve closest to shoulder and shoulder saddle, working under both strands of each edge st. K1, p2, k2, p2, k1 (saddle sts), pick up and k6 (6, 7, 8) sts to next pin. *NB: If you need to pick up more than 1 st in one of your edge sts, work under strand closest to you first, then work under both strands.* Small holes at these picked up sts are ok, as they form part of the design. Turn work. You will now work back and forth, adding sts on every row to shape the sleeve cap, maintaining the rib pattern at shoulder.

Part B:

Row 1: sl 1, p back, maintaining rib pattern at shoulder saddle. When you run out of sts, pm (first time only, to make counting easier), then pick up and **purl** (insert needle from the RS of work and draw yarn back through) 1 st. Always pick up new st in the very next edge st from the one previously worked. Turn work.

Row 2: sl 1, k to 2 sts before 1st p st at shoulder saddle; ssk, h-bar(k), p2, k2, p2, h-bar(k), k2tog. Knit to end, pm (1st time only), pick up and k1 st.

Row 3: Repeat Row 1.

Row 4: sl 1, k to shoulder saddle, p2, k2, p2, k to end, pick up and k 1 st.

Work these 4 rows until a total of 15 (18, 19, 20) sts have been added in each part B—50 (56, 60, 64) sts.

Part C:

Continue working back and forth, adding 1 st at the end of every row and making shoulder eyelets every 4 rows. When 6 (6, 7, 7) sts have been picked up at each end in section C between the marker and the held underarm sts, continue as follows:

WS Row: Work across to end, then p1 st from holder at underarm.

RS Row: Work across to end, then k1 st from holder.

Work these 2 rows until 6 sts are left on holder. You will now begin working in the round. Pm between the 2 knit sts at the underarm. This is the beginning of the round—80 (86, 94, 100) sts.

Maintaining the eyelet pattern at shoulder and repeating the same pattern at underarms, begin decs on next pattern Round 4 (non-eyelet round): k1, p2, k2tog, work in pattern to last 5 sts, ssk, p2, k1. Work decreases every 8th round 8 (8, 9, 9) more times, then every 4th round 7 (9, 10, 11) times. Continue working Sleeve as established until 14 (14½, 15, 16) in / 35.5 (37, 38, 40.5) cm from underarm, or 2½ in / 6.5 cm shorter than desired length. Knit 1 round, decreasing 0 (2, 6, 10) sts evenly—48 sts. Work k2, p2 ribbing for 6 in / 15 cm, bind off in pattern.

FRONT BAND

Using smaller 29 in / 80 cm circular needle and with RS facing, pick up and k50 (54, 60, 60) sts between bottom of sweater and the beginning of neck decs. Pick up 2 sts in corner edge st, pm. Continue to pick up and k along neck edge (1 st in every edge st); k across held sts at back of

neck. Pick up and k sts at left neck edge, pm, pick up 2 sts at corner, pick up and k50 (54, 60, 60) sts to end. Turn work. Work button band as follows:

Row 1 (WS): purl.

Rows 2 & 3: knit.

Row 4: purl.

Row 5: sl 1, *k2tog, yo; repeat from * to end. End row with k1 or k2, however many you have left.

Row 6: knit.

Row 7: purl.

Row 8 (buttonhole row): sl 1, k2 (2, 3, 3). Make buttonhole as follows: Wyif sl 1 st purlwise. *wyib sl 1, bind off by passing 1st slipped st over. Repeat from * 2 times. Slip the last bound-off st to the left needle. Turn work. Wyib cast on 4 sts by the cable cast on method (see Techniques). Turn work. Wyib sl 1, pass the last cast-on st over. Buttonhole complete. [K8 (9, 10, 10), make buttonhole] 4 times (5 buttonholes). Work to end of row.

Row 9: knit.

Row 10: purl.

Rows 11 & 12: knit.

Row 13: purl.

Using a larger needle (size 6 US / 4 mm or larger), bind off all sts.

FINISHING

Sew buttons on Left Front band. Weave in loose ends on wrong side of work.

For washing instructions read "Caring for Handknits" on page 114.

Saucy Sunhat

Designed by Eric Robinson. This quick and easy project offers a bit of warmth matched by a bit of ventilation, with lacy spirals in the crown and a broad brim to keep the ultraviolet rays at bay. It has plenty of "give" to fit various head sizes. Shown in Peony and Unbleached White Cotton Comfort.

SIZES: S/6–12 months (M/1–2 years, L/3–4 years)

FINISHED MEASUREMENTS

CIRCUMFERENCE: 15¼ (17, 19) in/39 (43, 48.5) cm

GAUGE: 21 sts, over 4 in/10 cm

MATERIALS

YARN: 1 skein of Cotton Comfort
NEEDLES: dpn, size 4 US/3.5 mm
OPTIONAL: size 4 US / 3.5 mm circular needle, 16 in / 40 cm long
  This hat is knit from the top down. As increases are worked and the hat grows, you may want to change to a circular needle.

TERMS USED

m1 = insert left needle from back to front under the bar between the st just worked and the next st and k this strand through the front

yo = yarn over

CROWN

Cast on 8 (9, 10) sts, distribute evenly on 3 dpn.
Join work, being careful not to twist sts.
Place marker for beginning of round.
Round 1: *yo, k1; repeat from *.
Rounds 2 & 3: knit.
Round 4: *yo, k2; repeat from *.
Rounds 5 & 6: knit.
Round 7: *yo, k3; repeat from *.
Rounds 8 & 9: knit.

Continue in this way until you complete round
25: *yo, k9—there are 80 (90, 100) sts.
Knit 2 rounds plain.

Eyelet round: *yo, k2tog, k8; repeat from *.
Knit 2 rounds plain.

Repeat Eyelet and 2 plain rounds 4 (5, 8) more
times, or until hat is desired length to brim (slip
sts onto a string to try on, if you like).

Next round:
S: *k2tog, k2tog, yo; repeat from *. 60 sts
M: *k2tog, k2tog, yo; repeat from *, end k2tog.
67 sts
L: *k2tog, k2tog, yo; repeat from *, end k2tog,
k2tog. 74 sts

Knit 1 round plain.

BRIM

First increase round:
S: *M1, k3; repeat from *. 80 sts
M: k1, *m1, k3; repeat from *, end m1. 90 sts
L: k1, *m1, k3; repeat from *, end m1, k1.
100 sts

All Sizes:
Knit 1 round plain, making following adjust-
ments: **S,** decrease 2 sts evenly; **L,** increase 2 sts
evenly.
Increase Round: *k6, m1; repeat from *.
Knit 3 rounds.
Inc. Round: *k7, m1; repeat from *.
Knit 3 rounds.
Inc. Round: *k8, m1; repeat from *.
Knit 3 rounds.
Inc. Round: *k9, m1; repeat from *.
Knit 5 rounds.

Work picot edge as follows:
Bind off 2 sts; *place remaining st back on left
needle; cast on 2; bind off 4*. Repeat from * to *
to the end. Is there an extra stitch? If so, bind it
off. Break yarn and pull through remaining st.

FINISHING

Weave in loose ends on wrong side of work.
Make a twisted or crochet cord or braid approximately 24 (27, 30) in / 60 (70, 80) cm long in
matching or contrasting yarn. Thread through
eyelets at base of crown and tie. After washing,
dry the hat over several loosely crumpled plastic
shopping bags; it will give the crown a nice
shape and allow you to smooth out the brim.

For washing instructions read "Caring for
Handknits" on page 114.

Islanders' Vest

Libby Mills designed this vest after a visit to Scotland's Outer Hebrides Islands, famous for their sheep and traditional knitting. The stitch pattern is based on Elizabeth Lovick's book Patterns for North Ronaldsay Yarn. *Liz named the design "Blanster" after a farm on South Ronaldsay Island mentioned in early medieval documents, which is still there today. Pictured in White Maine Organic.*

SIZES: XS (S, M, L)

FINISHED MEASUREMENTS
CHEST: 33 (38, 44, 49) in / 84 (97.5, 111, 124.5) cm
LENGTH TO UNDERARM: 11 (11, 13, 15) in / 28 (28, 33, 38) cm

GAUGE: 18 sts over 4 in / 10 cm

MATERIALS
YARN: 4 (5, 6, 6) skeins of Mountain Mohair OR 3 (3, 3, 4) skeins of Wonderfully Woolly or Vermont or Maine Organic
NEEDLES: size 5 US / 3.75 mm AND size 7 US / 4.5 mm circular needles, 29 in / 80 cm long
dpn, size 5 US / 3.75 mm AND size 7 US / 4.5 mm
NOTIONS: stitch holders, 6 (6, 7, 7) buttons, 2 markers, small safety pins

NB: The vest has a selvedge stitch at each end outside the pattern charts. These sts should be worked as follows throughout: on RS, slip first st as if to knit; k last st. On WS, slip first st as if to purl; p last st. It may be helpful to place markers next to these sts until you have established the pattern.

BODY

Using larger circular needle, cast on 149 (173, 197, 221) sts. Knit 2 rows. Work first pattern row: sl 1 (selvedge st), then work Row 1 of Chart A, k1 (selvedge st). Maintaining selvedge sts, work to Row 12 of Chart A, work Chart B, and repeat Chart A. On Row 12 of the 2nd Chart A, sl 1, k73 (85, 97, 109) sts, pm (place marker), k1, pm, work to end. The st between the markers is the center back st; the diagonals in Chart C reverse direction at this center st. Work Chart C, repeating Rows 2–5, until the piece measures 11 (11, 13, 15) in / 28 (28, 33, 38) cm or desired length to underarm, ending with a WS row.

Divide for front and back
Continuing in Chart C as established, work across 32 (37, 42, 47) sts for Right Front, bind off next 10 (12, 14, 16) sts, work across 65 (75, 85, 95) sts for Back; bind off next 10 (12, 14, 16) sts; work across 32 (37, 42, 47) sts for Left Front. Break yarn. Transfer Left and Right Front sts to holders or small circular needle.

Back: Beginning on WS, attach yarn and work one row in Chart C as established, reestablishing selvedge sts. On next RS row, begin decreases as follows: sl 1 (selvedge st), ssk, work to last 3 sts, k2tog, k1 (selvedge st). *NB: Do not work decrease sts in pattern.* Decrease 1 st each side every RS

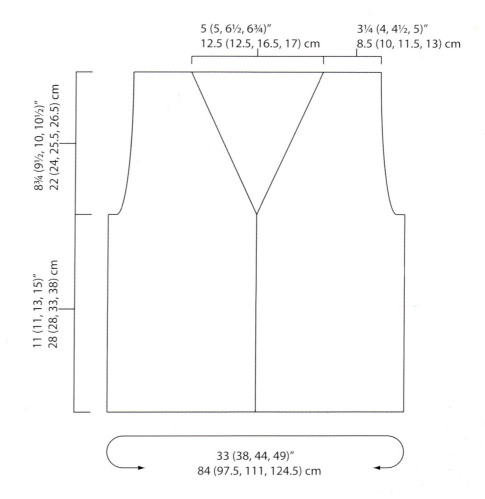

5 (5, 6½, 6¾)"
12.5 (12.5, 16.5, 17) cm

3¼ (4, 4½, 5)"
8.5 (10, 11.5, 13) cm

8¾ (9½, 10, 10½)"
22 (24, 25.5, 26.5) cm

11 (11, 13, 15)"
28 (28, 33, 38) cm

33 (38, 44, 49)"
84 (97.5, 111, 124.5) cm

row 3 (5, 7, 9) more times—57 (63, 69, 75) sts. AT THE SAME TIME, on the 3rd (4th, 5th, 7th) decrease row, work Chart A, continuing the selvedge sts (keep the center markers in place as they will be helpful with Chart D, but disregard them as you work Chart A). Row 6 of Chart A may not end at the end of the chart; make note of where you should start Row 7. After Chart A is finished, work Chart D, beginning at the point indicated for your size. *NB: Chart D will be the mirror image of Chart C.* Work even until

Back measures 8¾ (9½, 10, 10½) in / 22 (24, 25.5, 26.5) cm, ending with a WS row. Shape shoulders by working short rows as follows: work across 52 (57, 63, 67) sts; turn, sl 1, work 46 (50, 56, 58) sts; turn, sl 1, work 41 (44, 49, 50) sts; turn, sl 1, work 36 (38, 42, 42) sts; turn, sl 1, work 31 (32, 35, 34) sts; turn, sl 1, work 26 (26, 28, 26) sts; turn, sl 1, work in pattern to last 15 (18, 20, 24) sts, then k to end of row. Place 57 (63, 69, 75) sts on holder.

Chart A

Chart B

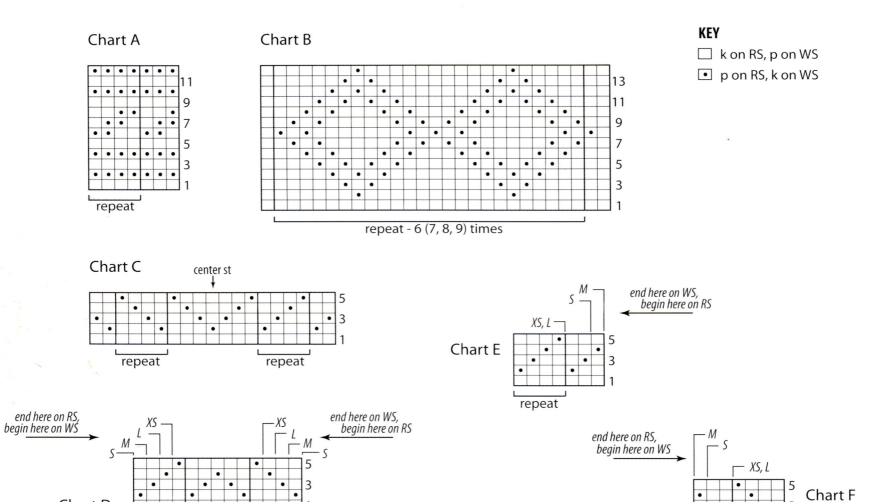

KEY

☐ k on RS, p on WS

⊡ p on RS, k on WS

Chart C

center st

repeat   repeat

Chart E

XS, L

S   M

end here on WS,
begin here on RS

repeat

Chart D

end here on RS,
begin here on WS

S   M   L   XS   XS   L   M   S

repeat   center st   repeat

end here on RS,
begin here on WS

M   S

XS, L

Chart F

repeat

Left Front: Transfer sts to needle. Continuing Chart C, work the next WS row, reestablishing selvedge sts. On next row begin decreases as follows: at armhole edge sl 1, ssk, work in pattern to last 3 sts, k2tog, k1. Place small safety pin at neck edge to mark beginning of decreases. Decrease 1 st at armhole edge every RS row 3 (5, 7, 9) more times. AT THE SAME TIME, dec 1 st at neck edge every 4th row 12 (12, 13, 13) more times.

Yoke Pattern: on the 2nd (4th, 6th, 10th) row after the last armhole decrease, work Chart A, making sure to continue neck decreases. *NB: This Chart A falls in a different spot vertically than on the Back.* Then work Chart E (begin at point indicated for your size, and repeat Rows 2–5), continuing neck decreases until 15 (18, 20, 23) sts remain. Work even until armhole measures same as Back. Shape shoulder with short rows as follows: (WS) work 10 (12, 14, 16) sts; turn, sl 1, work back to neck edge; turn, sl 1, work 4 (5, 6, 7) sts; turn, sl 1, work to neck edge; turn, sl 1, purl to end. Place sts on holder.

Right Front: Transfer sts to needle. Beginning at armhole edge on WS row, work to end of row in Chart C as established. On next row begin decreases as follows: sl 1, ssk, work in pattern to last 3 sts, k2tog, k1. Place small safety pin at neck edge. Work as for Left Front, reversing shaping, through Chart A. Then work Chart F, continuing neck decs until 15 (18, 20, 23) sts remain. Work even until armhole measures same as Back. Shape shoulder with short rows as follows: (RS) work 10 (12, 14, 16) sts; turn, sl 1,

work back to neck edge; turn, sl 1, work 4 (5, 6, 7) sts; turn, sl 1, work to neck edge; turn, sl 1, knit to end. Place sts on holder.

Turn vest inside out. Using the three-needle bind off (see Techniques), join left shoulder; then bind off 27 (27, 29, 29) Back neck sts and join right shoulder.

Front and Neck Band: Using smaller 29 in/80 cm circular needle and beginning at the bottom Right Front, pick up and k54 (54, 66, 78) sts to small safety pin; 35 (45, 55, 65) sts from safety pin to right shoulder seam; 22 (22, 29, 30) sts across back to left shoulder seam; 35 (45, 55, 65) sts from left shoulder seam to small safety pin; 54 (54, 66, 78) sts down left side. *Be sure to adjust these numbers if you have made the vest longer or shorter.* Next row: knit to small safety pin, inc 1; knit to left shoulder seam, k2tog; knit to right shoulder seam, k2tog; knit to safety pin, inc 1; knit to end. On next row make buttonholes: k2 (2, 2, 2) sts, ssk, k8 (8, 9, 11), ssk, k8 (8, 9, 11), ssk, *k8 (8, 8, 10), ssk; repeat from * 2 (2, 3, 3) times, pm, knit to end. On next row, k to marker, k1, yo, k9 (9, 10, 12), yo, k9 (9, 10, 12), yo, *k9, (9, 9, 11), yo; repeat from * 2 (2, 3, 3) times, k2. Bind off loosely purlwise.

Armbands: With RS facing and using smaller dpn, begin at underarm; pick up and k58 (85, 112, 139) sts, pm. *Purl one round, knit one round; repeat from * once. Bind off purlwise.

FINISHING

Weave in loose ends on wrong side of work. Sew on buttons.

For washing instructions read "Caring for Handknits" on page 114.

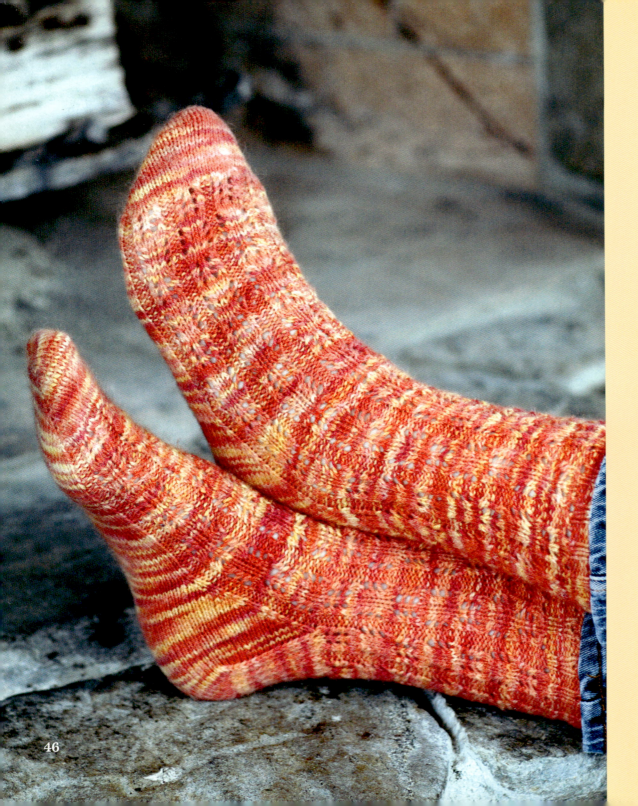

Wessagussett Wave Socks

Designed by Maureen Clark

The wavy lace pattern on these toe-up socks reminded Maureen of her favorite childhood beach.

SIZE: Women's M

GAUGE: 28 sts in stockinette st over 4 in / 10 cm

MATERIALS

YARN: 1 skein of Spinnery Sock Art Meadow or Forest

NEEDLES: size 1 US / 2.25 mm circular needle, 29 in / 80 cm long or longer (to make socks using the "Magic Loop" technique) OR
dpn, size 1 US / 2.25 mm
crochet hook, any size

TERMS USED

yo before a purl st = Wrap yarn forward between the needles, all the way around the right needle, and forward again for the next st.

W&T = Leaving working yarn where it is, slip next st purlwise, bring yarn between needles (to front or back), slip st back to left needle. Turn work.

kfb = increase by knitting into the front and back of st

Provisional cast on: Using waste yarn, crochet a chain of 35 sts. Then, with size 1 needle, pick up and knit 30 sts into back loops of chain.

Work stockinette short rows as follows:
Row 1: p to last st, W&T.
Row 2: k to last st, W&T.
Row 3: p to last unwrapped st, W&T.
Row 4: k to last unwrapped st, W&T.

Repeat Rows 3 & 4 until 8 unwrapped sts remain in center (11 wrapped sts at each end). On the next row, p9, W&T (double wrapped st). On the next row, k10, W&T. Continue in this way, knitting 1 more stitch on each row before W&T, until all outer stitches have been double wrapped.

Undo crochet chain, picking up 30 live sts on empty side of circular needle OR divide sts on 3 dpn: 30, 15, 15.

FOOT

Setup Round: k30 sole sts, work instep sts by [p2, k5] 4 times, p2.
Round 1: k sole sts, then [p2, k2tog, yo, k1, yo, ssk] 4 times, end p2 (Round 1 of Wave Pattern).
Round 2: k sole sts, then [p2, k5] 4 times, end p2 (Round 2 of Pattern).
Rounds 3–6: Repeat Rounds 1 and 2.
Rounds 7–8: Repeat Round 2.
Round 9: k sole sts, then [p2, yo, ssk, k1, k2tog, yo] 4 times, end p2 (Round 9 of Pattern).
Round 10: k sole sts, then [p2, k5] 4 times, end p2 (Round 10 of Pattern).
Rounds 11–14: Repeat Rounds 9 and 10.
Rounds 15–16: Repeat Round 10.

Repeat Rounds 1–16. When foot measures 3 in / 8 cm less than desired length, start gusset:
Round 1: kfb, k to 2 sts before end of sole sts, kfb, k1; work instep sts in pattern.
Round 2: knit sole sts, work instep sts in pattern. Repeat these 2 rounds for a total of 15 times (60 sole sts, 90 total sts).

NB: The next sections are worked with just the sole sts.

HEEL

Row 1: k43, W&T.
Row 2: p26, W&T.
Row 3: k24, W&T.
Row 4: p22, W&T.
Continue working short rows, 2 fewer sts each time, to k8, W&T.

HEEL FLAP

The 28 center sts are the heel flap; 16 sts on each end form the gusset.
Row 1: p17, working wraps together with st (pick up wrap from behind and place on left needle; purl together with the st). Purl last st together with first gusset st. Turn.
Row 2: sl 1, k26, knitting wraps together with sts, ssk with first gusset st.
Row 3: sl 1, p26, p2tog.
Row 4: sl 1, [k1, sl 1] 13 times, ssk.
Repeat Rows 3 & 4 until all gusset sts have been joined. On last row, after ssk, rejoin instep sts and work in pattern; increase 3 sts evenly across heel flap.

Wave Pattern

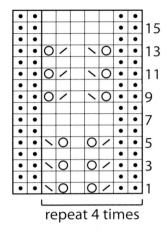

repeat 4 times

KEY
☐ knit
• purl
⊙ yo
⊘ k2tog
⊠ ssk

LEG

Work instep **and** heel flap sts in Wave Pattern for 7 in / 18 cm or desired length. End with Round 9 of Wave Pattern. Knit one round. Work k2, p2 rib for 1½ in / 4 cm. Then [k1, yo, k1, p2] around. On next round, [k3, p1, yo, p1]. Bind off loosely.

Make second sock the same as the first.

FINISHING
Weave in loose ends on wrong side of work.

For washing instructions read "Caring for Handknits" on page 114.

Jelly Beans Socks

Designed by Maureen Clark

These easy, textured socks have quickly become a favorite because of their great fit. Designed for Spinnery Sock Art, the stitch pattern is perfect for showing off variegated sock yarns.

SIZE: Women's M

GAUGE: 32sts over 4 in / 10 cm

MATERIALS

YARN: 1 skein of Spinnery Sock Art Meadow or Forest

NEEDLES: size 1 US / 2.25 mm circular needle, 29 in / 80 cm long or longer (to make socks using the "Magic Loop" technique) OR
dpn, size 1 US / 2.25 mm

TERMS USED

W&T = With yarn in back, slip next st purlwise, bring yarn between needles to front, slip st back to left needle. Turn work.

JELLY BEANS PATTERN

Rounds 1–3: k1, p1 around.
Rounds 4–6: p1, k1 around.
Repeat rounds 1–6 for Jelly Beans pattern.

KEY

☐   knit

⊡   purl

LEG

Cast on 64 sts. Join work, being careful not to twist sts. Work 12 rounds (6 ridges) garter stitch (k1 round, purl 1 round). Then work Jelly Beans Pattern until sock measures 5 in / 12.5 cm or desired length, ending with Round 3 or 6.

HEEL

You will now work back and forth across 32 heel stitches in garter stitch (knit every row). Shape the heel with short rows as follows: knit to last stitch; W&T. *NB: because you are working in garter stitch, there is no need to bring the yarn back between the needles.*

Repeat this last row once. On the next row, k29, W&T. On the next row, k28, W&T. Continue in this way, knitting 1 fewer stitch on each row before W&T, until 8 unwrapped stitches remain in the center of the needle (12 wrapped sts at each end)

On the next row, k9, W&T (double wrapped st). On the next row, k10, W&T. Continue in this way, knitting 1 more stitch on each row before W&T, until all outer stitches have been double wrapped.

FOOT

Resume working in the round: [k2, p1] across the heel stitches, ending k2. Then resume the Jelly Beans Pattern where you left off on the instep stitches. Continue in this manner, with instep sts in Jelly Beans Pattern and sole sts in k2, p1 rib until the sole measures 5½ in / 14 cm or 1½ in / 4 cm less than desired finished length, ending with the instep stitches.

TOE

Place the 32 instep stitches on one needle and divide the 32 sole stitches evenly on 2 needles. Change to garter stitch, starting with a purl round, and decrease as follows:
Round 1: p2tog at beginning of 1st heel needle and end of 2nd heel needle, and beginning and end of instep needle.
Round 2: knit.

Repeat these rounds until 24 stitches remain. Break yarn leaving a long tail and join toe stitches using the Kitchener stitch (see Techniques).

Make second sock the same as the first.

FINISHING
Weave in loose ends on wrong side of work.

For washing instructions read "Caring for Handknits" on page 114.

Alpine Lace Shell

Designed by Maureen Clark

This shell features a lace border inspired by Barbara Walker's design of the same name. A simpler lace borders neck and sleeve, contrasting nicely with the smooth stockinette body to create a season-spanning garment. Shown in Rose Quartz Sylvan Spirit.

SIZES: XS (S, M, L, XL)

FINISHED MEASUREMENTS

CHEST: in Sylvan Spirit: 36 (38, 40, 42½, 45¼) in / 91.5 (97, 102, 108.5, 115.5) cm
in Cotton Comfort: 36¼ (37¾, 40, 43, 45) in / 92.5 (96.5, 102, 109, 115) cm
LENGTH TO UNDERARM: 11½ in / 29.5 cm

This pattern is written for Sylvan Spirit and Cotton Comfort yarns, which work at slightly different gauges. For Sylvan Spirit, use the numbers in this typeface; *for Cotton Comfort, use the numbers in italics.*

GAUGE: for Sylvan Spirit, 24 sts over 4 in / 10 cm
for Cotton Comfort, 22 sts over 4 in / 10 cm
1 repeat (24 rows) of Alpine Lace Pattern = 2½ in / 6.5 cm

MATERIALS

YARN: 4 (4, 5, 5, 6) skeins of Sylvan Spirit or Cotton Comfort
NEEDLES: size 3 US / 3.25 mm circular needle, 16 in / 40 cm long
AND size 6 US / 4 mm circular needle, 29 in / 80 cm long
NOTIONS: 1 large and 2 small stitch holders

TERMS USED

k1b = knit into back of stitch
ssp = slip 2 sts, one at a time, as if to knit; return them together to the left needle and purl together through the back loops

For washing instructions read "Caring for Handknits" on page 114.

ALPINE LACE PATTERN—over 17 sts

(With thanks to Barbara Walker's *A Second Treasury of Knitting Patterns*)

A = k2, k1b, yo, k1, p2tog, yo 2 times, p2tog 2 times, yo—10 sts have been increased to 11.
B = k2, p2tog, yo, p2tog 2 times, yo 2 times, p2tog, yo, p2tog—12 sts have been decreased to 11. *NB: Some pattern rows begin with A and some with B.*

With smaller needle, cast on 17 sts and knit one row.

Row 1 (RS): k4, yo, p2tog, k2, yo, k2, p1, k3, yo, k1b, k2.

Row 2: A, k5, yo, p2tog, k2.

Row 3: [k4, yo, p2tog] 2 times, k1, p1, k3, yo, k1b, k2.

Row 4: A, k7, yo, p2tog, k2.

Row 5: k4, yo, p2tog, k6, yo, p2tog, k1, p1, k3, yo, k1b, k2.

Row 6: A, k9, yo, p2tog, k2.

Row 7: k4, yo, p2tog, k5, k2tog, yo, k1, yo, p2tog, k1, p1, k3, yo, k1b, k2.

Row 8: A, k3, yo, p2tog, k6, yo, p2tog, k2.

Row 9: k4, yo, p2tog, k3, k2tog, yo, k5, yo, p2tog, k1, p1, k3, yo, k1b, k2.

Row 10: A, k7, yo, p2tog, k4, yo, p2tog, k2.

Row 11: k4, yo, p2tog, k1, k2tog, yo, k9, yo, k3, p1, k3, yo, k1b, k2.

Row 12: k2, k1b, yo, k1, p2tog, yo 2 times, p2tog, p3tog, yo, k11, [yo, p2tog, k2] 2 times.

Row 13: k4, yo, p2tog, k2, yo, ssk, k7, k2tog, yo, k4, p1, p2tog, yo, p2tog, k2.

Row 14: k2, p2tog, yo, p2tog 2 times, yo 2 times, p2tog, k1, yo, p2tog, k5, ssp, yo, k5, yo, p2tog, k2.

KEY

☐	k on RS, p on WS
▧	p on RS, k on WS
ℓ	k into back of st
○	yarn over
╱	k2tog on RS, p2tog on WS
╲	ssk on RS, ssp on WS
◿	k3tog on RS, p3tog on WS
╱	p2tog on RS, k2tog on WS
■	no stitch

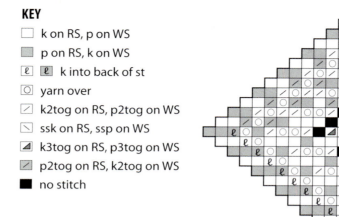

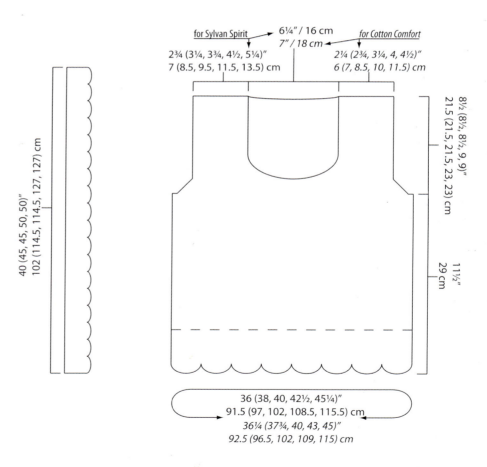

for Sylvan Spirit — 6¼" / 16 cm — for Cotton Comfort
7" / 18 cm

2¾ (3¼, 3¾, 4½, 5¼)"
7 (8.5, 9.5, 11.5, 13.5) cm

2¼ (2¾, 3¼, 4, 4½)"
6 (7, 8.5, 10, 11.5) cm

8½ (8½, 8½, 9, 9)"
21.5 (21.5, 21.5, 23, 23) cm

40 (45, 45, 50, 50)"
102 (114.5, 114.5, 127, 127) cm

11½"
29 cm

36 (38, 40, 42½, 45¼)"
91.5 (97, 102, 108.5, 115.5) cm

36¼ (37¾, 40, 43, 45)"
92.5 (96.5, 102, 109, 115) cm

Row 15: k4, yo, p2tog, k4, yo, ssk, k3, k2tog, yo, k1, p2tog, k1, p1, p2tog, yo, p2tog, k2.

Row 16: B, k1, ssp, yo, k7, yo, p2tog, k2.

Row 17: k4, yo, p2tog, k6, yo, k3tog, yo, k3, p1, p2tog, yo, p2tog, k2.

Row 18: B, k8, yo, p2tog, k2.

Row 19: k4, yo, p2tog, k5, k2tog, yo, k3, p1, p2tog, yo, p2tog, k2.

Row 20: B, k6, yo, p2tog, k2.

Row 21: k4, yo, p2tog, k3, k2tog, yo, k3, p1, p2tog, yo, p2tog, k2.

Row 22: B, k4, yo, p2tog, k2.

Row 23: k4, yo, p2tog, k1, k2tog, yo, k3, p1, p2tog, yo, p2tog, k2.

Row 24: B, k2, yo, p2tog, k2.

Work Rows 1–24 for a total of 16 (18, 18, 20, 20) times in Sylvan Spirit, *or 16 (16, 18, 18, 20) times in Cotton Comfort.* Bind off.

BODY

With RS of band facing and using smaller circular needle, pick up and k one st between each garter st ridge along the straight edge of lace— 192 (216, 216, 240, 240) / *192 (192, 216, 216, 240)* sts. Place marker for beginning of round. Join work and, with larger circular needle, purl one round. In the next round, increase 24 (12, 24, 16, 32) / *8 (16, 4, 20, 8)* sts spaced evenly—216 (228, 240, 256, 272) / *200 (208, 220, 236, 248)* sts. Work in stockinette st until piece measures 11½ in / 29.5 cm, or desired length to underarm.

Divide for front and back

Bind off 6 sts; k102 (108, 114, 122, 130) / *94 (98, 104, 112, 118)* sts for Back. Place the following 108 (114, 120, 128, 136) / *100 (104, 110, 118, 124)* sts on a large holder for Front.

BACK

Bind off 6 sts; purl the remaining 96 (102, 108, 116, 124) / *88 (92, 98, 106, 112)* sts.

Working back and forth, bind off 2 sts at the beginning of next 4 rows.

On the next row, decrease as follows: k1, k2tog, k to last 3 sts, ssk, k1.

Work decreases every other row 3 more times, then every 4th row 4 times—72 (78, 84, 92, 100) / *64 (68, 74, 82, 88)* sts. Work even until armhole measures 8½ (8½, 8½, 9, 9) in / *22 (22, 22, 23, 23) cm.* Place sts on large holder.

FRONT

Place Front sts on circular needle. With RS facing, join yarn and bind off 6 sts, knit across. Turn, bind off 6 sts, purl across. Bind off 2 sts at the beginning of the next 4 rows. On the next row, decrease as follows: k1, k2tog, k to last 3 sts, ssk, k1. Purl back.

Begin neck shaping:

Row 1: k1, k2tog, k36 (39, 42, 46, 50) / *32 (34, 37, 41, 44),* bind off 8 sts, k36 (39, 42, 46, 50) / *32 (34, 37, 41, 44),* ssk, k1.

Right Front

Row 2 and all even rows: working Right Front only, purl back.

Row 3: Bind off 4 sts at neck edge, k to last 3 sts, ssk, k1.

Row 5: Repeat Row 3.

Row 7: Bind off 3 sts, k to end.

Row 9: Bind off 2 sts, k to last 3 sts, ssk, k1.

Row 11: Bind off 2 sts, k to end.

Row 13: knit to last 3 sts, ssk, k1.

Row 15: knit

Row 17: knit to last 3 sts, ssk, k1.

Work even until armhole measures same as for Back. 17 (20, 23, 27, 31) / *13 (15, 18, 22, 25)* sts.

Left Front

Work as for Right Front, reversing shaping (sts will be bound off on WS rows).

Join Shoulders: Turn shell inside out and join shoulders using the three-needle bind off (see Techniques). Turn right side out.

NECK

Place the 38 sts from the holder onto larger circular needle. With RS facing, knit the 38 sts for Back neck, pick up and k 47 (47, 47, 50, 50) sts along side of neck, 8 sts from bound-off sts at center of neck, and 47 (47, 47, 50, 50) sts along 2nd side of neck.

Trim is the same for both yarns.

Round 1: purl.

Round 2: knit.

Round 3: *yo, p2tog; repeat from *.

Round 4: *k2tog, yo; repeat from *.

Round 5: purl.

Bind off all sts.

ARMBAND

Beginning at underarm, pick up and k 94 (94, 94, 100, 100) sts around armhole. Work trim the same as for neck band.

FINISHING

Weave in loose ends on wrong side of work. Sew ends of Alpine Lace band together.

Juliet Shell

Designed by Cap Sease

This pretty little top with an easy mock cable rib is knit from shoulders to hem for a custom fit. Shown in Sterling Sylvan Spirit.

FINISHED MEASUREMENTS

CHEST: 32 (34, 36, 38, 40) in / 81.5 (86.5, 91.5, 96.5, 101.5) cm

LENGTH TO UNDERARM: 12 (12½, 13, 13½, 13½) in / 30.5 (32, 33, 34.5, 34.5) cm

GAUGE: 24 sts in stockinette st over 4 in / 10 cm

MATERIALS

YARN: 3 (4, 4, 5, 5) skeins of Sylvan Spirit, Cotton Comfort, or Alpaca Elegance; waste yarn in worsted weight wool

NEEDLES: for Sylvan Spirit or Cotton Comfort, size 4 US / 3.5 mm circular needles, 16 in / 40 cm long AND 29 in / 80 cm long
dpn, size 4 US / 3.5 mm
for Alpaca Elegance, size 5 US / 3.75 mm circular needles, 16 in / 40 cm AND 29 in / 80 cm long
dpn, size 5 US / 3.75 mm long
size G / 4 mm crochet hook

NOTIONS: stitch holders, markers

MOCK CABLE STITCH

Round 1: *p2, k2; repeat from *, end k2.

Round 2: *p2, k1, yo, k1; repeat from *.

Round 3: *p2, k3; repeat from *.

Round 4: *p2, k3; with left needle pick up 1st
knit st on right needle; pass this st over 2nd
and 3rd knit sts and off needle; repeat from *.

Back: With waste yarn, crochet a chain of 85
(89, 97, 109) sts. Using project yarn and starting
on the 2nd chain st from the end of the chain,
pick up and k80 (84, 92, 96, 104) sts in the
back loops of chains. Work in stockinette st
until the back measures 6½ (7, 7½, 8, 8) in / 16.5
(18, 19, 20.5, 20.5) cm, ending with a WS row.
On next 4 RS rows, inc 1 st at each end—88
(92, 100, 104, 112) sts. Purl back. With RS facing, use cable cast on method to loosely cast on
10 sts. Place 98 (102, 110, 114, 122) Back sts
on holder.

Right Front: With waste yarn, crochet a chain
of 27 (27, 31, 31, 35) sts as for Back. Using project yarn and dpn, pick up and k22 (22, 26, 26,
30) sts in the chain. Work in stockinette st until
Front measures 5 (5½, 5½, 5½, 5) in / 12.5 (14,
14, 14, 12.5) cm, ending with a WS row. On
next 4 RS rows, inc 1 st at *end* of row—26 (26,
30, 30, 34) sts. After last inc, do not purl back.
Set work aside.

Left Front: Work as for Right Front until piece
measures 5 (5½, 5½, 5½, 5) in / 12.5 (14, 14, 14,
12.5) cm, ending with a WS row. On next 4 RS
rows, inc 1 st at *beginning* of row—26 (26, 30,
30, 34) sts. Purl back. Transfer sts to circular
needle.

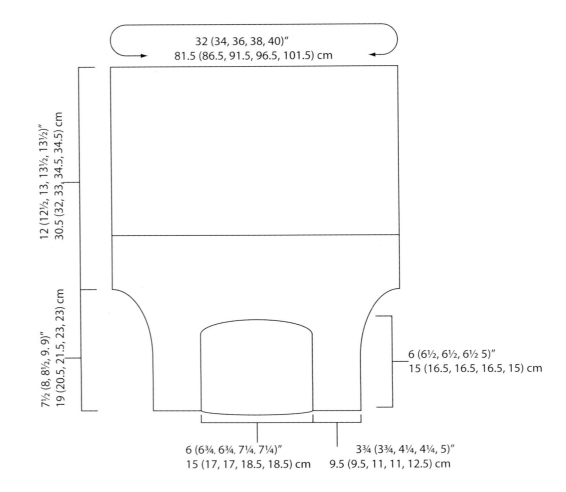

32 (34, 36, 38, 40)"
81.5 (86.5, 91.5, 96.5, 101.5) cm

12 (12½, 13, 13½, 13½)"
30.5 (32, 33, 34.5, 34.5) cm

7½ (8, 8½, 9, 9)"
19 (20.5, 21.5, 23, 23) cm

6 (6½, 6½, 6½ 5)"
15 (16.5, 16.5, 16.5, 15) cm

6 (6¾, 6¾, 7¼, 7¼)"
15 (17, 17, 18.5, 18.5) cm

3¾ (3¾, 4¼, 4¼, 5)"
9.5 (9.5, 11, 11, 12.5) cm

Join fronts as follows: With RS of the Left
Front facing, use the cable cast on method to
loosely cast on 28 (32, 32, 36, 36) sts for center
front. Turn work. Purl Right Front sts from dpn.
Work even on 80 (84, 92, 96, 104) sts until front
measures 6½ (7, 7½, 8, 8) in / 16.5 (18, 19, 20.5,
20.5) cm, ending with a WS row. On next 4 RS
rows, inc 1 st at each end—88 (92, 100, 104,
112) sts. Purl back. With RS facing, use cable
cast on method to loosely cast on 10 sts.

Join front and back: With RS facing, knit across
Front. Place Back sts on needle and knit across,
pm (place marker), and join work, being careful
not to twist sts. You will now work in the round
on these 196 (204, 220, 228, 244) sts. Work a
few rounds in stockinette st.

In order to custom fit the beginning of the ribbing, it will be helpful to join the shoulders as
follows: free the live stitches on the top of the

back by gently pulling the tail of the waste yarn. As the live sts are freed, place them on a needle. Then remove the waste yarn on both the front pieces and place the live sts on another needle. Beginning at an armhole edge, join first shoulder using the three-needle bind off (see Techniques). Bind off 36 (40, 40, 44, 44) Back sts, then join second shoulder as for the first.

Resume working on the body. To determine when to begin the mock cable ribbing, measure from the top of your shoulder to the point below your bust line where you would like the ribbing to start. When the vest measures the same distance from the shoulder seam, begin the Mock Cable Pattern. You can also try on the vest to make sure the pattern starts where you want it to. Beginning at the marker, work until the body measures 12 (12½, 13, 13½, 13½) in / 30.5 (32, 33, 34.5, 34.5) cm or desired length from underarm. Bind off loosely.

Neck edging: With shorter circular needle, pick up and k1 st in approximately every other st or row. On the next row, bind off as follows: *Bind off 2 sts. Turn work. Using the knit cast on method, cast on 3 sts. Turn work. Lift the 2nd, 3rd, and 4th sts one by one over the 1st st and off the needle.* Repeat from * to * until all sts have been bound off.

Armhole edging: Work as for Neck.

FINISHING
Weave in loose ends on wrong side of work.

For washing instructions read "Caring for Handknits" on page 114.

"*I became acquainted with the Spinnery decades ago through my great friendship with cofounder Libby Mills and have long enjoyed knitting and weaving with its high-quality yarns. It is difficult to find yarns that equal the quality and have the extensive color palette of the Spinnery yarns. I love them all! Over the last few years, it has been a treat, as well as a challenge, to support the Spinnery's mission by designing knitwear so others can enjoy the yarns as well.*"
CAP SEASE

Maureen's Cardigan

Designed by Maureen Clark.

This versatile cardigan falls just below the waist; it has indented sleeves and a V-neck with a small shawl collar that flatters any body type. This sweater dresses up or down with ease and will become a wardrobe staple. Shown in Pumpkin Wonderfully Woolly.

SIZES: S (M, L, XL)

FINISHED MEASUREMENTS

CHEST: 38 (40, 42, 44) in / 96.5 (101.5, 106.5, 112) cm
LENGTH TO UNDERARM: 11 in / 28 cm

GAUGE: 18 sts over 4 in / 10 cm, using larger needle

MATERIALS

YARN: 7 (8, 8, 8) skeins of Mountain Mohair OR 4 (4, 5, 5) skeins of Wonderfully Woolly or Vermont or Maine Organic
NEEDLES: size 7 US / 4.5 mm AND size 8 US / 5 mm circular needles, at least 24 in / 60 cm long
NOTIONS: markers, stitch holders, 6 buttons, approximately ⅝ in / 1.5 cm

BODY

Using smaller needle, cast on 172 (180, 192, 200) sts. Work 6 rows garter st (3 ridges on each side). Change to larger needle and stockinette st; work until piece measures 11 in / 28 cm, or desired length to underarm, ending with a WS row.

Divide for Armholes:

Knit 35 sts for Right Front, place these sts on a holder; bind off 16 (20, 26, 30) sts. Knit 70 sts for Back, place on holder; bind off 16 (20, 26, 30) sts. Knit 35 sts for Left Front.

Left Front: Purl one row. On the next row, k to last 3 sts, ssk, k1. Place a small safety pin at this edge to easily identify the first decrease row. Decrease in this way every 4th row 12 more times—22 sts. Work even until piece measures 9½ in / 24.5 cm from bound-off sts. Place sts on a holder.

Back: Beginning with a purl row, work even until Back is the same length as Left Front. Return sts to holder.

Right Front: Purl one row. On the next row, k1, k2tog, k to end of row. Place a small safety pin to easily identify the first decrease row. Decrease in this way every 4th row 12 more times—22 sts. Work even until piece measures the same as Left Front.

Join shoulders using the three-needle bind off (see Techniques).

Shawl Collar and Button Bands: Using smaller needle, begin at lower Right Front. Pick up and

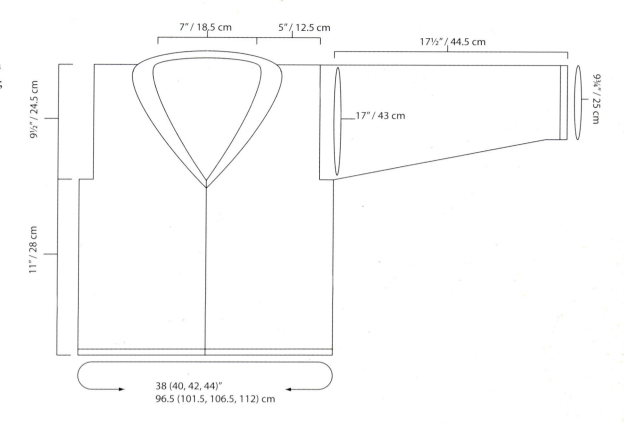

k51 sts to safety pin, pm (place marker) for neck. *NB: If you have made the sweater longer to the armholes, pick up an additional 4 or 5 sts for each additional inch between hem and neck marker, on both the Right and Left Fronts.* Pick up and k46 sts along neck edge; pick up and k the 26 bound-off sts across Back neck, increasing 6 sts evenly spaced for 32 sts. Pick up and k46 sts along Left neck edge to safety pin, pm for neck, pick up and k51 sts along Left Front.

Work garter st short rows as follows:
Row 1: Knit to first marker. Sm (slip marker), k27; place first shawl marker. K70, place second shawl marker. Turn work.

Row 2: knit to first shawl marker, remove marker, k1. Wrap next st (slip as if to purl, bring yarn to front), replace marker, then move slipped st back to left needle. Turn work.

Row 3: knit to second shawl marker, remove marker, k1. Wrap next st, replace marker, then move slipped st back to left needle. Turn work.

Repeat Rows 2 & 3 until all sts between the neck markers have been used. Complete row to bottom edge. Knit 2 more complete rows. On the following row work buttonholes as follows: k2, *yo, k2tog, k7; repeat from * 5 more times, k to end of row. *If you have more than 51 sts along* *front edges, be sure to adjust the spacing of button-holes to accommodate the extra length.* Knit 2 more rows. Bind off all sts.

SLEEVES *(make 2)*

With RS facing and using larger needle, pick up and k76 sts around armhole. Do not pick up the bound-off underarm sts. Work in stockinette st for 2 (2, 3, 3½, 4) in / 5 (5, 7.5, 8.5, 10) cm, ending with a WS row. Decrease 1 st at each end every 6th row 12 times; then every 4th row 4 times. Continue until sleeve measures 17 in / 43.5 cm, or desired length. Change to smaller needle and work 6 rows garter st. Bind off.

Beginning at underarm, join the first 2 (2, 3, 3½, 4) in / 5 (5, 7.5, 8.5, 10) cm of Sleeve to the bound-off sts for armhole; then sew remaining seam. Sew on buttons. Weave in loose ends on wrong side of work.

For washing instructions read "Caring for Handknits" on page 114.

The Lightweight Pullover

For children and adults

This versatile crew neck was initially designed to highlight our Cotton Comfort. Its simplicity allows any of our DK weight yarns to speak for themselves. Shown in Cocoa Alpaca Elegance, Citrine Sylvan Spirit, and Blue Opal Sylvan Spirit.

SIZES: child 2 (4, 6, 8, 10), *adult XS (S, M, L, XL)*

FINISHED MEASUREMENTS

CHEST: child—24 (26, 28, 30, 32) in / 61 (66, 71, 76, 81.5) cm
adult—34 (38, 42, 46, 50) in / 86.5 (96.5, 106.5, 117, 127) cm

LENGTH TO UNDERARM: child—8 (9, 10, 11, 12) in / 20.5 (23, 25.5, 28, 30.5) cm
adult—14 (15, 17, 18, 18) in / 35.5 (38, 43, 45.5, 45.5) cm

GAUGE: 20 sts over 4 in / 10 cm

MATERIALS

YARN: 3 (4, 4, 5, 5), *6 (8, 9, 9, 10)* skeins of Cotton Comfort, Sylvan Spirit, or Alpaca Elegance

NEEDLES: size 4 US / 3.5 mm AND size 6 US / 4 mm circular needles, 24 in / 60 cm long
size 4 US / 3.5 mm AND size 6 US / 4 mm circular needles, at least 29 in / 80 cm long
both child and adult—dpn, size 4 US / 3.5 mm AND size 6 US / 4 mm

NOTIONS: 3 large, 3 small stitch holders

Using smaller needle, cast on 120 (130, 140, 150, 160), *170 (190, 210, 230, 250)* sts. Place marker for beginning of round and join work, being careful not to twist sts. Work k1, p1 ribbing for 1½ in / 4 cm for child, *2 in/5 cm for adult.* Change to larger needle and work in stockinette st (k each round) until piece measures 8 (9, 10, 11, 12) in / 20.5 (23, 25.5, 28, 30.5) cm, *14 (15, 17, 18, 18) in/35.5 (38, 43, 45.5, 45.5) cm,* or desired length to underarm.

Divide for Armholes: knit 3 (4, 4, 4, 4), *6 (6, 7, 7, 7)* sts; place on a small holder. Knit 54 (57, 62, 67, 72), *73 (83, 91, 101, 111)* sts for Back; place remaining sts on large holder.

BACK

Working back and forth in stockinette st, continue until piece measures 5 (5½, 6, 6½, 7) in / 12.5 (14, 15, 16.5, 18) cm, *7¾ (8½, 9¼, 9¾, 10½) in / 20 (21.5, 23.5, 25, 27) cm* from dividing round, ending with a WS row. On the next row, k12 (13, 15, 17, 19), *19 (24, 27, 31, 35)* and place on a holder; bind off 30 (31, 32, 33, 34, 35), *35 (35, 37, 39, 41)* sts; k12 (13, 15, 17, 19), *19 (24, 27, 31, 35)* and place on a holder.

FRONT

Beginning with a RS row, k6 (8, 8, 8, 8), *12 (12, 14, 14, 14)* and place on a small holder. K54 (57, 62, 67, 72), *73 (83, 91, 101, 111)* for Front and place remaining 3 (4, 4, 4, 4), *6 (6, 7, 7, 7)* sts on a small holder. Work even until piece measures 3 (3½, 4, 4½, 5) in / 7.5 (9, 10, 11.5, 12.5) cm, *5½ (6½, 6½, 7, 8) in/14 (16.5, 16.5, 18, 20.5) cm.*

To shape neck, k16 (17, 19, 21, 23), *24 (29, 32, 37, 41)*; bind off 22 (23, 24, 25, 26), *25 (25, 27, 27, 29)*; k16 (17, 19, 21, 23), *24 (29, 32, 37, 41).* Purl back, attaching a second ball of yarn for left side of neck. On next row, decrease as follows: on left side of neck k to last 4 sts, k2tog, k2. On right side of neck, k2, ssk, k to end. Decrease in this way every RS row 3 (3, 3, 3, 3), *4 (4, 4, 5, 5)* more times. Work even on both sides until Front measures same as Back. Leave sts on needle.

Join shoulders using the three-needle bind off (see Techniques).

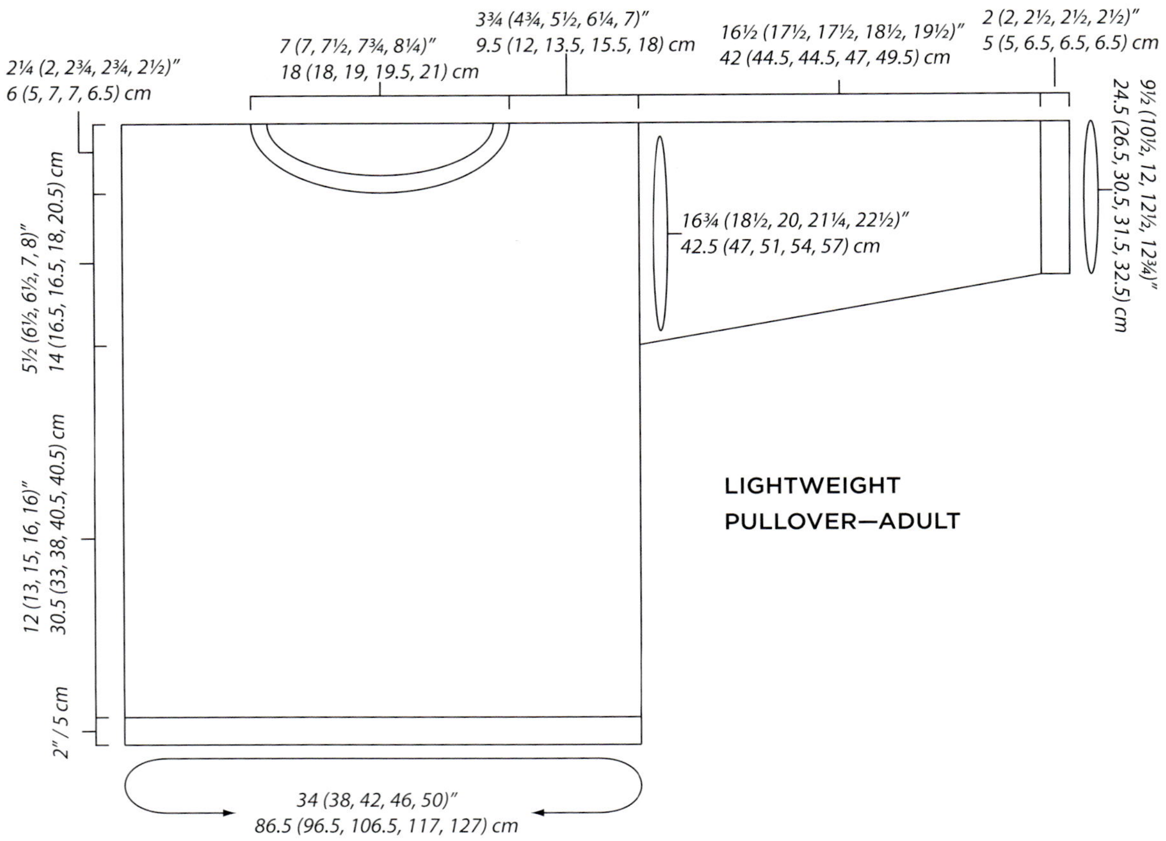

2¼ (2, 2¾, 2¾, 2½)"
6 (5, 7, 7, 6.5) cm
7 (7, 7½, 7¾, 8¼)"
18 (18, 19, 19.5, 21) cm
3¾ (4¾, 5½, 6¼, 7)"
9.5 (12, 13.5, 15.5, 18) cm
16½ (17½, 17½, 18½, 19½)"
42 (44.5, 44.5, 47, 49.5) cm
2 (2, 2½, 2½, 2½)"
5 (5, 6.5, 6.5, 6.5) cm
9½ (10½, 12, 12½, 12¾)"
24.5 (26.5, 30.5, 31.5, 32.5) cm
16¾ (18½, 20, 21¼, 22½)"
42.5 (47, 51, 54, 57) cm
5½ (6½, 6½, 7, 8)"
14 (16.5, 16.5, 18, 20.5) cm
12 (13, 15, 16, 16)"
30.5 (33, 38, 40.5, 40.5) cm
2"/5 cm
34 (38, 42, 46, 50)"
86.5 (96.5, 106.5, 117, 127) cm

LIGHTWEIGHT PULLOVER—ADULT

NECK

With RS facing and smaller dpn, pick up and k30 (31, 32, 33, 34), *35 (35, 37, 39, 41)* sts across Back neck; pick up and k11 sts along side of neck for child, *13 (13, 13, 17, 17) sts along side of neck for adult;* pick up and k22 (23, 24, 25, 26), *25 (25, 27, 27, 29)* sts across Front neck; pick up and k11 sts along side of neck for child, *13 (13, 13, 17, 17) sts along side of neck for adult*—74 (76, 78, 80, 82), *86 (86, 90, 100, 104)* sts. Work k1, p1 ribbing for ¾ in / 2 cm for child, *1 in/2.5 cm for adult.* Bind off in ribbing.

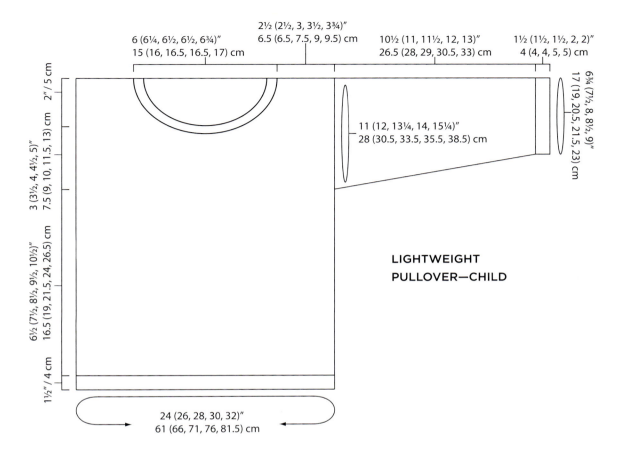

6 (6¼, 6½, 6½, 6¾)"
15 (16, 16.5, 16.5, 17) cm

2½ (2½, 3, 3½, 3¾)"
6.5 (6.5, 7.5, 9, 9.5) cm

10½ (11, 11½, 12, 13)"
26.5 (28, 29, 30.5, 33) cm

1½ (1½, 1½, 2, 2)"
4 (4, 4, 5, 5) cm

6¾ (7½, 8, 8½, 9)"
17 (19, 20.5, 21.5, 23) cm

2" / 5 cm

3 (3½, 4, 4½, 5)"
7.5 (9, 10, 11.5, 13) cm

11 (12, 13¼, 14, 15¼)"
28 (30.5, 33.5, 35.5, 38.5) cm

6½ (7½, 8½, 9½, 10½)"
16.5 (19, 21.5, 24, 26.5) cm

1½" / 4 cm

**LIGHTWEIGHT
PULLOVER—CHILD**

24 (26, 28, 30, 32)"
61 (66, 71, 76, 81.5) cm

SLEEVES *(make 2)*

Using larger dpn and with RS facing, place 3 (4, 4, 4, 4), *6 (6, 7, 7, 7)* sts from holder onto needle and knit them; pick up and k48 (52, 58, 62, 68), *72 (80, 86, 92, 98)* sts along armhole edge; place 3 (4, 4, 4, 4), *6 (6, 7, 7, 7)* sts from second holder onto needle and knit them—54 (60, 66, 70, 76), *84 (92, 100, 106, 112)* Sleeve sts. Working in stockinette st, decrease 1 st each end of round every 1 in / 2.5 cm 8 (8, 8, 8, 7), *9 (12, 12, 8, 8)* times, then every ¾ in / 2 cm 1 (1, 3, 3, 6), *7 (5, 5, 11, 13)* times—36 (42, 44, 48, 50), *52 (60, 66, 68, 70)* sts. Work even until Sleeve measures

10½ (11, 11½, 12, 13) in / 26.5 (28, 29, 30.5, 33) cm, *16½ (17½, 17½, 18½, 19½) in / 42 (44.5, 44.5, 47, 49.5) cm,* or 1½ (1½, 1½, 2, 2) in / 4 (4, 4, 5, 5) cm, *2 (2, 2½, 2½, 2½) in / 5 (5, 6.5, 6.5, 6.5) cm* less than desired length. On the next round, decrease 2 (4, 4, 5, 5), *4 (6, 6, 6, 6)* sts evenly. Change to smaller dpn and work k1, p1 rib for 1½ (1½, 1½, 2, 2) in / 4 (4, 4, 5, 5) cm, *2 (2, 2½, 2½, 2½) in / 5 (5, 6.5, 6.5, 6.5) cm.* Bind off in ribbing.

FINISHING

Weave in loose ends on wrong side of work.

For washing instructions read "Caring for Handknits" on page 114.

Leafy Lace Shawl

Designed by Cap Sease

This easy introduction to lace knitting yields a dramatic stole, shawl, or scarf. Shown in Antique Brass Sylvan Spirit.

FINISHED MEASUREMENTS

LENGTH: 80 in / 203 cm

WIDTH: 18 in / 46 cm

For a wider shawl, cast on 8 more sts (one pattern repeat) for every 2 in/5 cm you wish to increase the width. For a narrower shawl or scarf, reduce the number of cast-on sts by 8 for every 2 in/5 cm you wish to decrease the width.

GAUGE: 16 sts in pattern over 4 in / 10 cm after blocking

MATERIALS

YARN: 5 skeins of Sylvan Spirit, Alpaca Elegance, or Cotton Comfort

NEEDLES: size 9 US / 5.5 mm circular or straight needles crochet hook (optional)

TERMS USED

yo = yarn over

sl = slip as if to knit

sl 1, k2tog, psso = double decrease: slip 1, k2tog, pass the slipped st over the k2tog

LACE PATTERN—*multiple of 8 + 1*

Rows 1 & 3 (WS): sl 1 as if to purl, purl to end.

Row 2: sl 1, *k2tog, yo, k3, yo, ssk, k1; repeat from *.

Row 4: sl 1, k2, *yo, sl 1, k2tog, psso, yo, k5; repeat from *, ending k3.

Cast on 65 sts loosely. Begin Lace Pattern. Repeat Rows 1–4 until piece measures 80 in / 203 cm or desired length. Bind off loosely.

Twisted Fringe (optional): Make lark's head knots on each end of shawl as follows: Cut 14 in / 36 cm lengths of yarn. Holding two pieces together, fold them in half; using a crochet hook, pull the loop through a st in the cast-on edge. Then pull the ends through the loop and tighten to form a knot. Repeat, evenly spaced, along cast-on edge, and then along bound-off edge. To twist the fringe, hold one strand of yarn in each hand. Twist each strand clockwise until the yarn begins to kink. Hold the strands together and twist them counterclockwise. Tie an overhand knot at the end to hold the twist. Repeat. Trim fringe ends so they are even.

pattern repeat

KEY

☐   purl on WS, knit on RS

∨   slip stitch

╱   k2tog

◯   yarn over

╲   ssk

⅄   sl 1, k2tog, psso

FINISHING

Weave in loose ends on wrong side of work. Wash gently by hand in warm water with mild detergent. Rinse gently in warm water. Then roll in a towel to remove excess moisture, or spin in washing machine for 10 seconds. Lay flat on a large towel to dry, pinning to correct dimensions.

Laurie Gilbert has been running the carding machine for more than 15 years. He compares it to "flying a World War I biplane—it's the same age—perhaps not quite as dangerous."

Meadow Lark Lace

An elegant, easy lace pattern designed by Melissa Johnson. Equally lovely as a scarf or shawl, this pattern lends itself particularly well to subtle handpainted colorways. The pointed ends can be embellished with beads or tassels if desired.

FINISHED MEASUREMENTS

LENGTH: Scarf—72 in / 183 cm, Shawl—82 in / 208 cm
WIDTH: Scarf—7½ in / 19 cm, Shawl—22½ in / 57 cm

GAUGE: Approximately 26 sts in pattern over 4 in / 10 cm

MATERIALS

YARN: One skein Spinnery Sock Art Meadow or Forest for Scarf, 3 skeins for Shawl
NEEDLES: Size 6 US / 4 mm straight or circular needles

LACE PATTERN—*multiple of 10 + 1*

Row 1 (WS): purl.

Row 2: k1, *yo, k3, k3tog, k3, yo, k1; repeat from *.

Row 3: knit.

Row 4: same as Row 2.

INSTRUCTIONS

Loosely cast on 51 (151) sts. Work in Lace Pattern until piece measures 72 in / 183 cm (82 in / 208 cm), ending with Row 1. On the next row bind off loosely in knit.

FINISHING

Weave in loose ends. Wash gently by hand in warm water with mild detergent. Rinse gently in warm water. Then roll in a towel to remove excess moisture, or spin in washing machine for 10 seconds. Lay flat on a large towel to dry, pinning to correct dimensions.

Lace Pattern

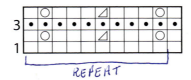

REPEAT

KEY

☐ knit on RS, purl on WS

⊡ purl on RS, knit on WS

◎ yarn over

◿ knit 3tog

Great Meadows Cardigan

Designed by Melissa Johnson

Inspired by sweaters and textiles from her childhood, Melissa has created this classic children's V-neck cardigan for knitting in a rich yet easy Fair Isle pattern or a solid color with contrasting trim. Sitting at her worktable, Melissa looks out to the Great Meadows, rich agricultural land on the banks of the Connecticut River. Shown in Mountain Mohair: Moss, Rhubarb, Claret, and Mesa.

SIZES: 2 (4, 6, 8, 10)

FINISHED MEASUREMENTS

CHEST: 24 (26, 28, 30, 32) in / 61 (66, 71, 76, 81.5) cm
LENGTH TO UNDERARM: 9 (9½, 10, 10½, 11) in / 23 (24, 25.5, 26.5, 28) cm

GAUGE: 18 sts and 24 rows in stockinette st, over 4 in / 10 cm on larger needle

MATERIALS

YARN: Wonderfully Woolly
  Solid Version: 1 (2, 3, 3, 3) skeins color A, 1 skein color B
  Fair Isle Version: 1 (1, 2, 2, 2) skeins color A
  1 skein each in colors B, C and D
  OR
  Mountain Mohair
  Solid Version: 2 (4, 5, 5, 6) skeins color A
  1 (1, 2, 2, 3) skeins color B
  Fair Isle Version:
  2 (2, 2, 3, 3) skeins color A
  1 (1, 1, 2, 2) skeins in colors B and C
  1 skein color D

NEEDLES: size 6 US/4 mm AND size 8 US/5 mm
circular needles, 29 in/80 cm long
2 straight needles, size 8 US/5 mm or smaller
NOTIONS: 1 large, 2 medium stitch holders
BUTTONS: 4 (5, 5, 6, 7) approximately ⅝ in/
1.5 cm

For washing instructions read "Caring for
Handknits" on page 114.

BODY is worked in one piece to the armholes.
With smaller needle and color B, cast on 105
(117, 123, 135, 141) sts. Work 7 rows garter
stitch (knit each row). Change to larger needle
and color A. Working in stockinette st, follow
chart for Fair Isle version, or continue in color A
for solid version. *NB: When working in Fair Isle,
be sure to carry both colors in use to the last st in
each row. If the color needed for next row is at the
other end of needle, slide sts to that end and knit or
purl as appropriate to continue in stockinette st.*
Work straight until body measures 9 (9½, 10,
10½, 11) in/23 (24, 25.5, 26.5, 28) cm, or
desired length to underarm.

Divide for Armholes: With RS facing, knit 22
(25, 24, 27, 29) sts for Right Front and place on
holder. Bind off 9 (9, 13, 13, 13) sts for underarm, k43 (49, 49, 55, 57) sts for Back and place
on holder, bind off 9 (9, 13, 13, 13) sts for
underarm, knit 22 (25, 24, 27, 29) sts for Left
Front.

Left Front: purl one row. On the next row begin
neck decreases as follows: k19 (22, 21, 24, 26),
k2tog, k1. Continue to work decrease every 4th
row 4 (4, 5, 5, 5) more times, then every other
row until 12 (13, 12, 14, 13) sts remain. Work

COLORWAYS FOR FAIR ISLE VERSION:

Wonderfully Woolly

Color	I	II	II
A	Strawberry	Teal	White
B	Trillium	Deep Lake	Fiddlehead
C	Chestnut	Eggplant	Pine Warbler
D	Pine Warbler	Fiddlehead	Teal

Mountain Mohair

Color	IV	V	VI
A	Moss	Partridgeberry	Ice Blue
B	Mesa	Raspberry	Sky Blue
C	Rhubarb	Claret	Pink Pink
D	Claret	Midnight Blue	Day Lily

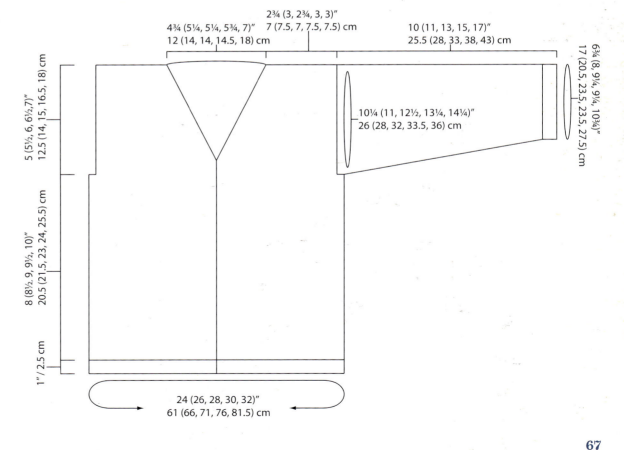

straight until armhole measures 5 (5½, 6, 6½, 7) in / 12.5 (14, 15, 16.5, 18) cm. *Be sure to knit armhole to indicated measurement so that sleeves will fit properly. For Fair Isle version, some sizes will end partway through a motif; however, a pleasing pattern will result when shoulders are joined.* Place stitches on holder.

Right Front: Attach yarn at armhole and purl one row. On the following row, begin decreasing for neck: k1, ssk, work to end of row. Continue decreasing every 4th row and then every other row as for Left Front. Work to same measurement as Left Front and place sts on holder.

Back: Beginning with a purl row, work until back measures 5 (5½, 6, 6½, 7) in / 12.5 (14, 15, 16.5, 18) cm above dividing round. With sweater inside out, place the 12 (13, 12, 14, 13) sts for left front shoulder on one needle and an equal number for back left shoulder on a second needle. Join with three-needle bind off (see Techniques). Repeat for second shoulder. Leave remaining sts on holder for back neck.

SLEEVES *(make 2)*
With smaller needle and color B cast on 30 (36, 42, 42, 48) sts. Work 7 rows in garter st. Change to larger needle and color A. Follow Fair Isle chart for sleeve, or continue in A for solid version, increasing every 6th row as follows: k1, m1, k to 1 st before end of row, m1, k1. Continue increases until there are 46 (50, 56, 60, 64) sts. Work straight until sleeve measures 10 (11, 13, 15, 17) in / 25.5 (28, 33, 38, 43) cm, or desired length. Bind off loosely.

Front Band: With smaller needle and color B,

pick up and k3 sts for every 4 rows along Right Front and neck edge; k sts from holder for Back neck; pick up and k3 sts for every 4 rows along Left Front and neck edge. Work 3 rows garter st. Mark 4 (5, 5, 6, 7) evenly spaced locations for buttonholes along right edge for girls, left edge for boys. On the following row bind off 2 sts at each location. On the next row, cast on 2 sts over each space.

Work three more rows of garter st. Bind off all sts, being careful not to work too tightly.

Pockets for Solid Sweater (optional): With

Color A and larger needle, cast on 15 (15, 19, 19, 23) sts. Work in stockinette st until pocket measures 3 (3½, 3½, 4, 4) in / 7.5 (9, 9, 10, 10) cm. Change to color B and smaller needle and work 4 rows of garter st; bind off. Make second pocket to match. Sew onto lower fronts of sweater.

FINISHING
Beginning at underarm, join the first 1 (1, 1½, 1½, 1½) in / 2.5 (2.5, 4, 4, 4) cm of Sleeve to the bound-off sts at underarm; then sew remaining seam. Sew on buttons. Weave in loose ends on wrong side of work.

Body Chart

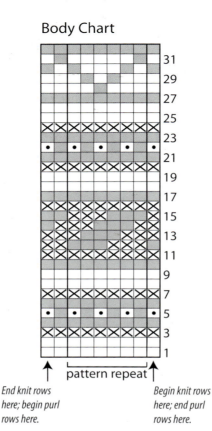

End knit rows here; begin purl rows here.

pattern repeat

Begin knit rows here; end purl rows here.

Sleeve Chart

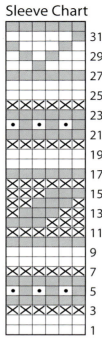

KEY

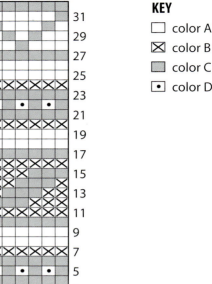

☐ color A
☒ color B
▨ color C
⊡ color D

Great Meadows Hat

Designed by Melissa Johnson

Perfect as a first Fair Isle project or to try out a colorway for the companion Great Meadows Cardigan, this hat is colorful, fun, and easy to knit. Shown in Wonderfully Woolly (Iris, Turquoise, Teal, and Fiddlehead).

SIZES: S (M, L)

FINISHED MEASUREMENTS

CIRCUMFERENCE: 18½ (20, 21½) in /47 (51, 54.5) cm

GAUGE: 18 sts and 24 rows in pattern, over 4 in /10 cm.

MATERIALS

YARN: 1 skein each of 4 colors of Mountain Mohair or Wonderfully Woolly

NEEDLES: size 8 US /5 mm circular needle, 16 in /40 cm long dpn, size 8 US /5 mm
size E /3.5 mm crochet hook

See Great Meadows Cardigan pattern for suggested Colorways.

With circular needle and color B, cast on 84 (90, 96) sts. Join work, being careful not to twist sts, and place marker for beginning of round. Work garter st (purl one round, knit one round) for 7 rounds. Work pattern chart. After completing chart, with color A work 4 rounds garter st. Next Round: *p1, k13 (14, 15); repeat from *. Repeat this round two more times.

Decrease

Round 1: *p1, k11 (12, 13), k2tog; repeat from *.
Round 2: *p1, k12 (13, 14); repeat from *.
Round 3: *p1, k10 (11, 12), k2tog; repeat from *.
Round 4: *p1, k11 (12, 13); repeat from *.
Round 5: *p1, k9 (10, 11), k2tog; repeat from *.
You will now begin decreasing every round.
Round 6: *p1, k8 (9, 10), k2tog; repeat from *.
Round 7: *p1, k7 (8, 9), k2tog; repeat from m*.
Continue decreasing every round as established until 12 sts remain. On last round, k2tog all around. Cut yarn, leaving a 20 in / 50 cm tail. Using a tapestry needle, thread yarn through remaining sts and pull together firmly. If desired, use tail to crochet in chain st for 5 in / 12.5 cm and attach a tassel to the end.

FINISHING
Weave in loose ends on wrong side of work.

For washing instructions read "Caring for Handknits" on page 114.

Hat Chart

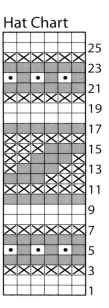

KEY

- ☐ color A
- ☒ color B
- ▨ color C
- ⊡ color D

Country Cable Cardigan

Designed by Maureen Clark while on a journey to the Wisconsin Sheep and Wool Festival, this sweater travels from town to country with ease. Shown in Deep Lake Wonderfully Woolly.

SIZES: XS (S, M, L)

FINISHED MEASUREMENTS

CHEST: 36 (40, 44, 48) in / 91.5 (101.5, 112, 122) cm
LENGTH TO UNDERARM: 12 (12, 13, 14) in / 30.5 (30.5, 33.5, 36) cm
SLEEVE LENGTH TO UNDERARM: 15½ (16, 17¼, 18½) in / 39.5 (41, 44, 47) cm

GAUGE: 24 sts and 30 rows in pattern, over 4 in / 10 cm. Row gauge is important for raglan shaping.

MATERIALS

YARN: 6 (7, 7, 8) skeins of Wonderfully Woolly or Vermont or Maine Organic OR
10 (11, 12, 14) skeins of Mountain Mohair
NEEDLES: size 7 US / 4.5 mm circular needle, 24 in / 60 cm long
dpn, size 7 US / 4.5 mm
NOTIONS: cable needle, markers, 5 medium stitch holders
BUTTONS: 7, approximately ½ in / 1.5 cm

TERMS USED

k1b = knit into back of stitch
m1 = insert left needle from back to front under the bar between the st just worked and the next st and k this strand through the front

CABLE PATTERN *(over 12 sts)*

Row 1: *Slip 2 sts onto cn (cable needle) and
hold in back of work, k2, k2 sts from cn, k4,
slip 2 sts onto cn and hold in front, k2, k2 sts
from cn; repeat from *

Rows 2, 4, 6, & 8: purl

Rows 3 & 7: knit

Row 5: *k2, slip 2 sts onto cn and hold in front,
k2, k2 sts from cn, slip 2 sts onto cn and hold
in back, k2, k2 sts from cn, k2; repeat from *.

Repeat Rows 1–8 for Cable Pattern.

INSTRUCTIONS

BODY

Cast on 182 (204, 224, 246) sts on circular needle. Do not join. Work back and forth in ribbing
as follows:

Row 1 (RS): k1b, p1.

Row 2 (WS): k1, p1.

Repeat these 2 rows for 1½ in / 4 cm.
Work next 2 rows as follows:

1: Knit all sts, increasing 20 (22, 26, 28) sts
evenly across row for a total of 202 (226, 250,
274) sts.

2: P49 (55, 61, 67), k1, p1, pm (place marker),
p1, k1, p96 (108, 120, 132), k1, p1, pm, p1,
k1, p49 (55, 61, 67). This row creates the two
underarm "seams."

Begin Cable Pattern:

RS Rows: k1, work cable pattern over 48 (54,
60, 66) sts, p1, k1b, sm (slip marker), k1b, p1,
cable pattern over 96 (108, 120, 132) sts, p1,
k1b, sm, k1b, p1, cable pattern over 48 (54, 60,

66) sts, k1. *NB: For sizes 40 and 48 the cable
pattern on the front will end in the middle of the
pattern; start the back and second front in the cable
pattern where you left off, making the pattern match
on each side of each "seam."*

WS Rows: p49 (55, 61, 67), k1, p1, sm, p1, k1,
p96 (108, 120, 132), k1, p1, sm, p1, k1, p49 (55,
61, 67).

Continue in this manner until work measures 12
(12, 13, 14) in / 30.5 (30.5, 33.5, 36) cm or
desired length to underarm, ending on Row 2 or
6. Set aside.

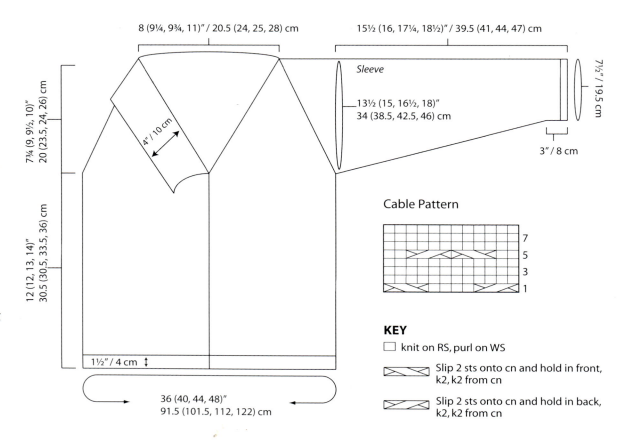

8 (9¼, 9¾, 11)" / 20.5 (24, 25, 28) cm

15½ (16, 17¼, 18½)" / 39.5 (41, 44, 47) cm

Sleeve

7½" / 19.5 cm

13½ (15, 16½, 18)"
34 (38.5, 42.5, 46) cm

4" / 10 cm

7¾ (9, 9½, 10)"
20 (23.5, 24, 26) cm

3" / 8 cm

12 (12, 13, 14)"
30.5 (30.5, 33.5, 36) cm

1½" / 4 cm

36 (40, 44, 48)"
91.5 (101.5, 112, 122) cm

Cable Pattern

7

5

3

1

KEY

☐ knit on RS, purl on WS

⬚ Slip 2 sts onto cn and hold in front,
k2, k2 from cn

⬚ Slip 2 sts onto cn and hold in back,
k2, k2 from cn

SLEEVES *(make two)*

With dpn, cast on 46 sts. Join work, being careful not to twist sts. Work ribbing for 1 in / 3 cm
as follows:

Round 1: k1b, p1.

Round 2: k1, p1.

Work next 2 rounds as follows:

Round 1: Knit all sts, increasing 8 sts evenly for a
total of 54 sts.

Round 2: K1, p1, k50, p1, k1.

*NB: Since sleeves are worked in the round, even-
numbered rounds in the cable pattern will now be
knit.*

Begin Cable Pattern: k1b, p1, k1, work pattern to last 3 sts, k1, p1, k1b.

Continue in this manner for 2 in / 5 cm. On next round and every following 6th (5th, 4th, 4th) round, increase 1 st on each side of the "seam" sts as follows: k1b, p1, m1, work Cable Pattern to last 2 sts, m1, p1, k1b. Incorporate increased sts into Cable Pattern when possible. Continue increasing for a total of 13 (18, 23, 27) times—80 (90, 100, 108) sts; then work even until sleeve measures 15½ (16, 17¼, 18½) in / 39.5 (41, 44, 47) cm or desired length to underarm, ending on Round 1 or 5. On next round, work to last 8 (8, 10, 10) sts and place next 16 (16, 20, 20) sts on holder.

JOIN WORK

On Body work in pattern to 8 (8, 10, 10) sts before marker, place next 16 (16, 20, 20) sts on holder; work across first Sleeve, maintaining pattern; work across Back to 8 (8, 10, 10) sts before marker, place next 16 (16, 20, 20) sts on holder; work across second Sleeve; work to end of row—298 (342, 370, 410) sts. Purl back.

Establish raglan "seams": On next row k1, work 40 (46, 50, 56) sts in Cable Pattern, p1, k1b, pm, k1b, p1; work 60 (70, 76, 84) sts in pattern, p1, k1b, pm, k1b, p1; work 80 (92, 100, 112) sts in pattern, p1, k1b, pm, k1b, p1; work 60 (70, 76, 84) sts, p1, k1b, pm, k1b, p1; work to end in pattern, ending with k1.

Maintaining pattern, decrease 1 st (p2tog—one st from body with p st from raglan "seam") before and after each raglan "seam" every other row 27 (30, 35, 38) times, then every 4th row 1 (2, 0, 0) times. AT THE SAME TIME, begin

decreasing for neck as follows: on RS, k1, ssk, work to last 3 sts, k2tog, k1. Decrease for neck again on next RS row, then every 4th row 11 (13, 14, 18) times. Put remaining 48 (56, 58, 66) sts on holder for collar.

BUTTON BANDS

With RS facing, pick up and knit 70 (70, 75, 80) sts on Left Front between neck shaping and bottom of sweater. *NB: If your sweater is longer or shorter than suggested, you will need more or fewer sts.*

Work in twisted rib as for bottom of sweater for 1½ in / 4 cm. Bind off. On Right Front, pick up and k sts as for Left Front and work ribbing for ¾ in / 2 cm; work 7 buttonholes (k2tog, yo) evenly spaced; work ribbing until even with Left Band. Bind off.

COLLAR

With RS facing, pick up and knit 66 (70, 76, 82) sts along right neck edge, 48 (56, 58, 66) sts from holder and 66 (70, 76, 82) sts along left neck edge. Work these 180 (196, 210, 230) sts in k1b, p1 rib for 2½ in / 6.5 cm. On next RS row, increase as follows: work 60 (68, 72, 82) sts, *m1, k1, m1, k5. Repeat from * 10 (10, 11, 11) more times, then complete row. Work another 1½ in / 4 cm, incorporating increased sts into ribbing. Bind off.

FINISHING

Join underarm seams with Kitchener stitch (see Techniques). Weave in loose ends on wrong side of work. Sew on buttons.

For washing instructions read "Caring for Handknits" on page 114.

Snowy Woods Sweater

This pullover by Cap Sease recalls the designs of the early-twentieth-century Bohus Stickning knitting collective of Sweden. The interplay of brown, black, and grey with the white reminded Cap of woodlands on an early winter's day.

SIZES: P (XS, S, M, L, XL)

FINISHED MEASUREMENTS

CHEST: 34 (36, 40, 44, 48, 52) in /86.5 (91.5, 101.5, 112, 122, 132) cm

LENGTH TO UNDERARM: 14 (14, 14½, 16, 16½, 16¾) in /35.5 (35.5, 37, 41, 42, 42.5) cm

GAUGE: 20 sts over 4 in /10 cm

MATERIALS

YARN: Alpaca Elegance—4 (6, 7, 8, 9, 10) skeins Main Color (MC), 1 skein each of 3 Contrasting Colors (A, B, C)

NEEDLES: Size 6 US /4 mm circular needles, 16 in / 40 cm AND 29 in /80 cm long

BODY

With longer circular needle and MC cast on 172 (180, 200, 220, 240, 260) sts. Pm (place marker) for beginning of round and join work, being careful not to twist sts.

Work 4 rounds garter stitch (knit 1 round, purl 1 round).

Work Chart 1, then continue in Stockinette st with MC until the Body measures 14 (14, 14½, 16, 16½, 16¾) in / 35.5 (35.5, 37, 41, 42, 42.5) cm, ending 4 (5, 5, 5, 7, 7) sts before marker.

Divide for Front and Back: place 8 (10, 10, 10, 14, 14) sts on holder for underarm, work 78 (80, 90, 100, 106, 116) sts for Front, place 8 (10, 10, 10, 14, 14) sts on holder, work 78 (80, 90, 100, 106, 116) sts for Back. Set aside.

SLEEVES *(make 2)*

Using dpn, cast on 40 (48, 52, 52, 56, 60) sts. Join work, being careful not to twist sts. Pm for beginning of round. Work 4 rounds garter st, then work Chart 1. Work in MC until sleeve measures 2 in / 5 cm. Increase 1 st at beginning and end of every 6th round 11 (0, 0, 3, 11, 12) times; then every 8th round 0 (9, 10, 10, 4, 4) times—62 (66, 72, 78, 86, 92) sts. Work even until sleeve measures 15½ (16¾, 17¾, 19, 20¼, 20½) in / 39.5 (42.5, 45, 48.5, 51.5, 52) cm, ending 4 (5, 5, 5, 7, 7) sts before marker. Place the next 8 (10, 10, 10, 14, 14) sts on a holder or piece of waste yarn. Place the remaining sts on holder and set aside.

Join sleeves and body as follows: Using yarn attached to body and with RS facing, knit across 54 (56, 62, 68, 72, 78) sts of one Sleeve, 78 (80, 90, 100, 106, 116) sts of Front, 54 (56, 62, 68, 72, 78) sts of other Sleeve, 78 (80, 90, 100, 106, 116) sts of Back—264 (272, 304, 336, 356, 388) sts. On next round, dec 4 (2, 4, 1, 1, 3) sts evenly—260 (270, 300, 335, 355, 385) sts. Work straight until yoke measures 2 (2, 2¼, 2½, 2½, 2¾) in / 5 (5, 5.5, 6.5, 6.5, 7) cm from joining round.

Decrease Round 1: With MC *k3, k2tog; repeat from * around—208 (216, 240, 268, 284, 308) sts. Knit 1 round. Work Chart 1. Knit one round MC, decreasing 4 (0, 0, 4, 2, 2) sts evenly. Work Chart 2.

Knit one round MC *increasing* 4 (0, 0, 4, 2, 2) sts evenly. Repeat Chart 1.

Dec Round 2: With MC *k2, k2tog; repeat from * around—156 (162, 180, 201, 213, 231) sts. Knit 1 round MC. Knit 1 round MC, decreasing 0 (0, 0, 1, 1, 1) st. Work Chart 3. Knit 2 rounds MC. Knit 1 round MC, *increasing* 0 (2, 0, 0, 4, 2) sts. Work Chart 1. Knit 1 round MC, decreasing 0 (2, 0, 2, 3, 1) sts.

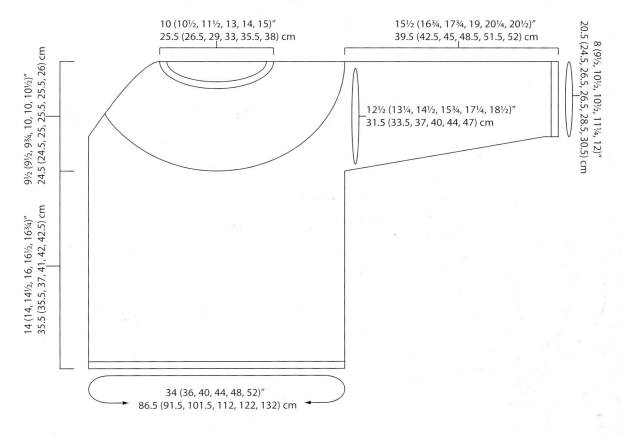

10 (10½, 11½, 13, 14, 15)"
25.5 (26.5, 29, 33, 35.5, 38) cm

15½ (16¾, 17¾, 19, 20¼, 20½)"
39.5 (42.5, 45, 48.5, 51.5, 52) cm

8 (9½, 10½, 11¼, 11¾, 12)"
20.5 (24.5, 26.5, 26.5, 28.5, 30.5) cm

12½ (13¼, 14½, 15¾, 17¼, 18½)"
31.5 (33.5, 37, 40, 44, 47) cm

9½ (9½, 9¾, 10, 10, 10½)"
24.5 (24.5, 25, 25.5, 25.5, 26) cm

14 (14, 14½, 16, 16½, 16¾)"
35.5 (35.5, 37, 41, 42, 42.5) cm

34 (36, 40, 44, 48, 52)"
86.5 (91.5, 101.5, 112, 122, 132) cm

Dec Round 3: *k1, k2tog; repeat from *—104 (108, 120, 132, 142, 154) sts

In MC, work 6 rounds garter st, beginning with a purl round. Bind off.

FINISHING

Join underarm seams using the Kitchener stitch (see Techniques). Weave in loose ends on wrong side of work.

For washing instructions read "Caring for Handknits" on page 114.

KEY   *change colors as indicated on Charts*

☐ knit

• purl

☑ slip purlwise, with yarn in back

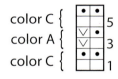

Chart 1

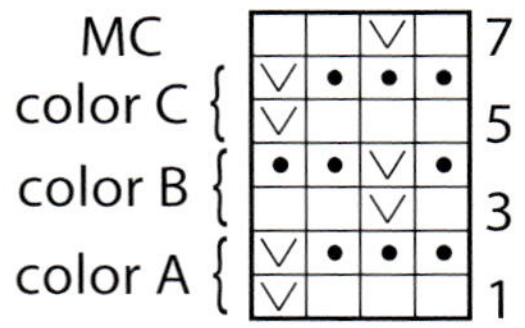

MC
color C {
color B {
color A {

Chart 2

color A {
color C {
color A {

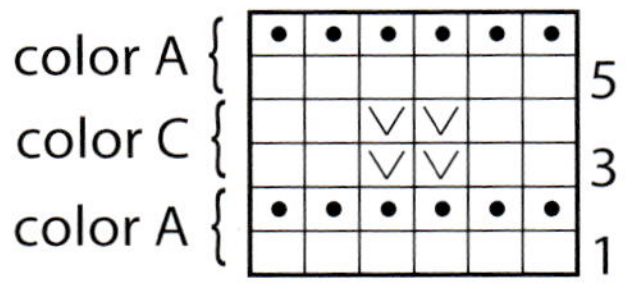

Chart 3

color C {
color A {
color C {

Turkish Rose Mittens

Designed by Cap Sease

The pattern on these mittens comes from an ancient pair of Turkish stockings and is called gul, Turkish for "rose." The motif may remind you of climbing roses or a meandering garden path. Shown in White and Cappuccino Alpaca Elegance.

SIZES: S (M, L)

FINISHED MEASUREMENTS

HAND LENGTH: 7 (8, 9) in / 18 (20.5, 23) cm from top of cuff

HAND WIDTH: 4 (4½, 5) in / 10 (11.5, 12.5) cm

GAUGE: 28 sts and 28 rows over 4 in / 10 cm on larger needles

MATERIALS

YARN: 1 skein each of 2 colors of Alpaca Elegance

NEEDLES: dpn, size 0 US / 2 mm AND size 2 US / 2.75 mm

NOTIONS: 2 markers, waste yarn

CUFF

With smaller needles and color B cast on 54 (60, 63) sts. Join work, being careful not to twist sts, and work k2, p1 rib for 10 (12, 14) rounds. Work Cuff Chart. (If you wish, you can make up your own striped design.)

HAND

Change to larger needles and stockinette st. Knit one round with color A, increasing 4 (6, 7) sts evenly—58 (66, 70) sts.

Right Mitten: Beginning Rose Chart at the arrow for your size, work 29 (35, 35) sts in chart, k1 B, pm (place marker). Beginning with A, work 5 sts in Checkerboard Pattern, pm, continue Checkerboard Pattern to end of round. *NB: The sts between the markers are the thumb gusset. The gusset marker sts (the B sts outside the stitch markers) will always be worked in B. At times there may be several B sts in a row.*

Work Rounds 2–4 of Rose Chart, maintaining the Checkerboard Pattern over the thumb gusset and palm and keeping the gusset marker sts in B.

Round 5: Work in pattern to 1st marker, sm (slip marker), m1 B, k5, m1 B, sm, k1 B, continue Checkerboard Pattern to end. Continue Rose Chart, increasing 1 st inside each marker every other round (in the appropriate color for the Checkerboard Pattern) until there are 15 (17, 19) sts between the markers. Work even until mitten measures 2½ (2¾, 3) in / 6.5 (7, 8) cm from top of cuff.

KEY
☐ color A
▩ color B

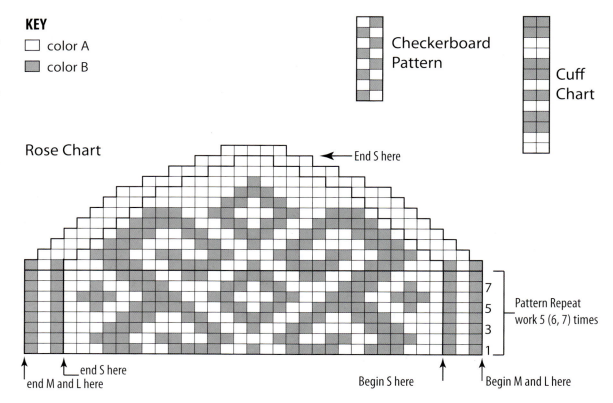

Checkerboard Pattern

Cuff Chart

Rose Chart

← End S here

7
5
3
1

Pattern Repeat
work 5 (6, 7) times

↑ end S here
↑ end M and L here

↑ Begin S here
↑ Begin M and L here

Next round: Work to 1st marker, place 15 (17, 19) gusset sts on waste yarn. Maintaining Checkerboard Pattern, use the backward loop method to cast on 5 sts over the gap, then continue to end. Incorporate the gusset marker sts into the Checkerboard Pattern on this round or the next, whichever maintains the pattern. Continue as established until you have completed 5 (6, 7) repeats of the Rose Chart.

Decrease: Maintaining patterns as established, work next round of chart, dividing sts on needles as follows: **S**—29, 15, 14; **M**—35, 16, 15; **L**—35, 18, 17.

Decrease Round 1: Needle 1—K1 A, ssk, work to last 3 sts, k2tog, k1 A.
Needle 2—K2tog, work to end.
Needle 3—Work to last 2 sts, ssk.
Repeat this round 6 more times.

Decrease Round 2: Needle 1—K1 A, ssk, k2tog, work to last 5 sts, k2tog, k2tog, k1 A.
Needles 2 & 3—K2tog, work to last 2 sts, ssk.
Repeat this round 1 (2, 2) more times.

For small size only:
Decrease Round 3: Needle 1—K1 A, ssk, k1, k2tog, k1 A.
Needle 2—K2tog, work to last 2 sts, ssk.

Needle 3—K2tog, k1—9 sts.

For medium & large:
Decrease Round 3: Needle 1—K1 A, ssk, k2tog, k1, k2tog, k1 A.
Needle 2—K2tog, work to last 2 sts, ssk.
Needle 3—K2tog, k1—11 sts.

Break yarns. Using a tapestry needle, thread yarn through remaining sts and pull together firmly.

THUMB

Place 15 (17, 19) gusset sts on needle. Maintaining Checkerboard Pattern, pick up and k2 sts at one side of the thumb hole, 6 sts along the cast-on edge, and 2 sts on other side of thumb hole—25 (27, 29) sts.

Divide sts evenly on needles. Work in Checkerboard Pattern until thumb measures 1¾ (2, 2) in / 4.5 (5, 5) cm, or ½ in / 1.5 cm less than desired length.

Decrease thumb tip as follows:
Round 1: On each needle k2tog, work to last 2 sts, ssk.
Round 2: knit.
Repeat these two rounds 2 (2, 3) more times—7 (9, 5) sts.

Break yarns. Using a tapestry needle, thread yarn through remaining sts and pull together firmly.

Left Mitten: Knit the cuff and one round in A with increases as for Right Mitten.
Next Round: Work 29 (35, 35) sts of Rose. Chart. Beginning with B, work Checkerboard Pattern to last 6 sts. Place 1st marker. Maintaining Checkerboard Pattern, k5, pm, k1 B. Continue as for Right Mitten.

FINISHING
Weave loose ends in on wrong side of work.

For washing instructions read "Caring for Handknits" on page 114.

Anatolian Flip

Designed by Eric Robinson

Is it a hat or is it a bag? This easy two-color pattern is knit as a tube, with no shaping. The Turkish pattern, called Poppy, is symmetrical, which makes following the chart a breeze. Knit it in two or more colors and finish it off with tassels and braids. A fun project for Mountain Mohair or Wonderfully Woolly.

SIZES: S (M, L)

FINISHED MEASUREMENTS

CIRCUMFERENCE: 18 (19½, 21) in / 46 (50, 53.5) cm

GAUGE: 22 sts and 22 rows in pattern over 4 in / 10 cm

MATERIALS

YARN: 1 skein Main Color (MC), 1 skein each desired Contrasting Color (CC) in Mountain Mohair or Wonderfully Woolly

NEEDLES: size 7 US / 4.5 mm circular needle, 16 in / 40 cm long

TERMS USED

2-color long tail cast on = Using 1 strand of MC and 1 strand of CC held together, tie a slipknot and place on needle. (This knot will be removed later and does not count as a st.) With MC over thumb and CC over finger, cast on desired number of sts, then take slipknot off and join work.

Some hints about following the Poppy Pattern Chart: This design is absolutely symmetrical and each round is basically very simple; you may find that, with the exception of the first few stitches and the center of the pattern, you can memorize the sequence in most rounds (2 MC, 2 CC, 2 MC, 2 CC, etc.). Read every round of the chart from right to left. Be aware that the center of the chart is the fold line for the finished hat/bag.

Cast on 100 (108, 116) sts, using a 2-color long tail cast on with MC over thumb and CC over finger. Join work, being careful not to twist sts.

Round 1: *Work first 41 sts of Round 1 of Poppy Chart, pm (place marker). K1 in CC, then work last 4 chart sts 2 (3, 4) times, pm*. Repeat from * to *. Following chart and changing CC as desired, work through round 44 (48, 53) of Poppy Chart or to desired length. Piece should measure approximately 8 (8½, 9) in / 20.5 (22, 23) cm from cast-on round.

Work braided edge with MC and one CC:

Round 1: k1 MC, k1 CC.

Round 2: Move both yarns to front. P1 MC, p1 CC, always bringing new color **under from the left.** *NB: Your 2 yarns will twist around each other during this process. Don't try to untwist them; simply pull out a healthy amount of yarn and keep going, as they will untwist on the next round.*

Round 3: p1 MC, p1 CC, always bringing new color **over from the right.**

Round 4: Bind off in k, maintaining color pattern.

ANATOLIAN FLIP

Poppy Pattern Chart

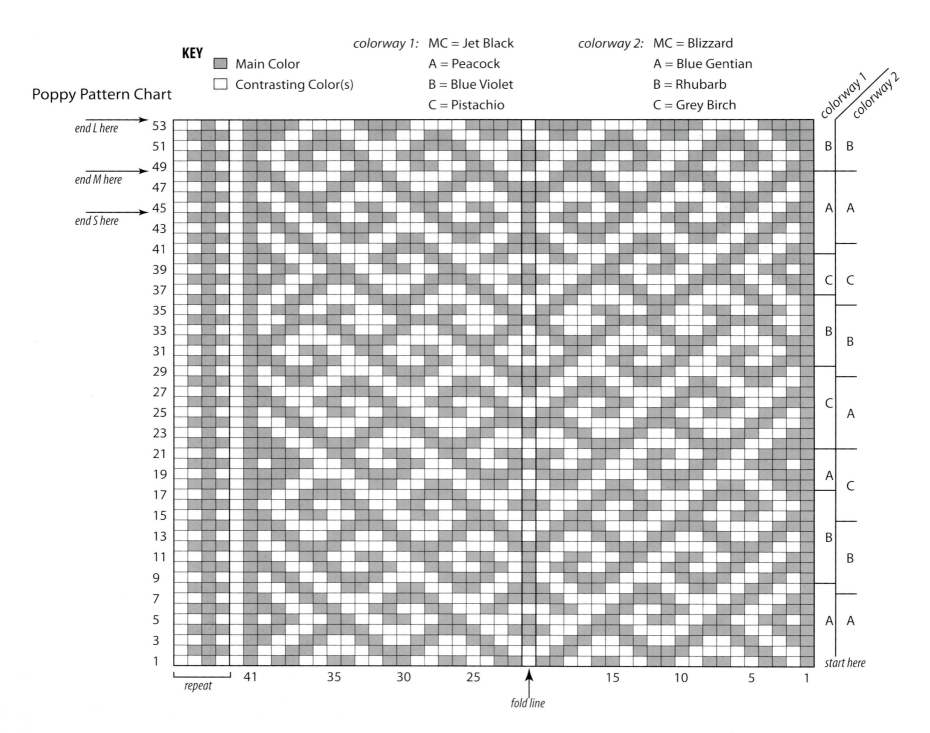

end L here → 53
51
end M here → 49
47
end S here → 45
43
41
39
37
35
33
31
29
27
25
23
21
19
17
15
13
11
9
7
5
3
1

repeat   41   35   30   25   fold line   15   10   5   1

colorway 1 / colorway 2

B B
A A
C C
B B
C A
A C
B B
A A

start here

FINISHING

Fold piece in half along fold line. Sew cast-on edges together with MC and overcast st. Make 2 tassels in desired colors and attach to corners. To make braid ties, wrap yarn to make a thin tassel, but don't cut or tie off. Cut 12 pieces of yarn approximately 60 in / 150 cm long in desired colors (we used 4 each of 3 CC) and thread 6 of those strands through the tassel as if to tie it. Fold this yarn in half so you have 12 strands and braid it loosely to the end. Tie end of braid in an overhand knot to secure. At other end, finish off tassel. Make second braid to match. At braided edge of hat / bag, carefully stretch a hole between the braid and the Poppy Pattern, then poke the knotted end of braid through from the inside and pull until the ends are even. Trim ends. To use as a bag, pull the knotted ends, allowing the tassels to slip inside, and tie together.

Weave in loose ends on wrong side of work.

For washing instructions read "Caring for Handknits" on page 114.

Riley's Hat

Designed by Maureen Clark

Originally created for Maureen's new grandson, this retro-styled hat with earflaps ties under the chin to stay on through all sorts of winter fun. Shown in Sylvan Spirit (Blue Opal and Rose Quartz).

SIZES: S/3–6 months (M/6–12 months, L/1–2 years, XL/2–5 years)

FINISHED MEASUREMENTS

CIRCUMFERENCE: 14 (15, 17, 19) in/35.5 (38, 43, 48.5) cm

GAUGE: 24 sts in stockinette st over 4 in/10 cm

MATERIALS

YARN: 1 (1, 2, 2) skeins of Alpaca Elegance, Cotton Comfort, New Mexico Organic, or Sylvan Spirit

NEEDLES: size 4 US/3.5 mm circular needle, 16 in/40 cm long

dpn, size 4 US/3.5 mm

Cast on 84 (92, 100, 112) sts. Place marker for beginning of round; join work, being careful not to twist sts.

Work k2, p2 ribbing for 3½ (4, 4, 4) in / 9 (10, 10, 10) cm. Switch to stockinette st and work for 3½ (4, 4, 4) in / 9 (10, 10, 10) cm. On the next round, decrease 3 (11, 4, 0) sts evenly—81 (81, 96, 112) sts. Work 1 round even.

Top decreases:
Round 1: *ssk, k7 (7, 10, 12); repeat from *.
Round 2 & all even rounds: knit.
Round 3: *ssk, k6 (6, 9, 11); repeat from *.
Round 5: *ssk, k5 (5, 8, 10); repeat from *.

Continue decreasing in this way, with one fewer st between decreases to *ssk, k1. Knit 1 round; end with *ssk around. Break yarn, leaving 10 in / 25 cm. Using a tapestry needle, thread yarn through remaining sts and pull together firmly.

EARFLAPS *(make 2)*
Turn hat inside out and find the center rib line (where your rounds began). Beginning at the 3rd set of k sts to the left of center, pick up and k18 (22, 26, 26) sts at the juncture between ribbing and stockinette st. Work k2, p2, rib for 2 in / 5 cm (make sure you are beginning with k2 on the RS of the flap). Work following RS rows (hat ribbing facing you): k1, ssk, rib to last 3 sts, k2tog, k1. WS rows: k the knits and p the purls. Work until 4 sts remain. On next RS row k1, k2tog, k1.

Ties: Work I-cord (see Techniques) for 6 in / 16 cm or desired length. On next row k1, k2tog, pass st over as if to bind off (1 st left). Break yarn and pull through remaining st.

Make second earflap the same, spacing it the same distance from center back

FINISHING
Weave in loose ends on wrong side of work. Make a pom-pom or tassel and attach to top.

For washing instructions read "Caring for Handknits" on page 114.

Melissa's Hat & Mittens

These elegant patterns designed by Melissa Johnson are a great introduction to two-color knitting. The many possible combinations will keep you intrigued through numerous projects.

SIZES: S (M, L) The small size will fit a large child.

FINISHED MEASUREMENTS

HAT CIRCUMFERENCE: 18½ (20, 21½) in /47 (51, 54.5) cm

MITTEN (AROUND HAND ABOVE THUMB): approximately 6 (7¾, 9¼) in /15 (19.5, 23.5) cm

GAUGE: *for hat*—24 sts over 4 in /10 cm
for mittens—26 sts over 4 in /10 cm

MATERIALS

YARN: 1 skein in each of 4 colors in Cotton Comfort, Sylvan Spirit, or Alpaca Elegance

NEEDLES: *for hat*—size 5 US /3.75 mm circular needle, 16 in /40 cm long AND dpn, size 5 US /3.75 mm
for mittens—dpn, size 3 US /3.25 mm

OPTIONAL: size E /3.5 mm crochet hook

NOTIONS: small stitch holder

TERMS USED

sl 1, k2tog, psso = double decrease—slip 1, k2tog, pass the slipped st over

	Cotton Comfort	Sylvan Spirit	Alpaca Elegance	
A	Silver	Luminosity	White	Dark Roast
B	Weathered Green	Amethyst	Cappuccino	White
C	Denim	Blue Opal	Charcoal	Charcoal
D	Storm	Peridot	Dark Roast	Cocoa

HAT INSTRUCTIONS

Using circular needle and color D, cast on 110 (120, 130) sts. Join work, being careful not to twist sts. Work Cuff Chart.

When cuff is complete, work Pattern Chart until hat is approximately 2¾ in / 7 cm less than desired length, ending with Round 5. On the following round, k2 A, k1 B and place a marker on the needle. This is now the beginning of the round.

Setup round for Decrease Chart: Beginning at marker, *k1 A, k1 B, k7 A, k1 B; repeat from * 10 (11, 12) times. Work one more repeat, ending with k8 A.

Decrease Chart: Each round of the Decrease Chart begins at the marker. Repeat the sts on the chart 11 (12, 13) times. Decreases are made by k2tog where indicated. Change to dpn when necessary. After completing chart, cut yarn, leaving 20 in / 51 cm of color B. Using a tapestry needle, thread yarn through remaining sts and pull together firmly.

If desired, crochet a 3 in / 8 cm chain using the color B tail and attach a small tassel in color D to end of chain.

EARFLAPS (optional)

Leaving a space of about 5 in / 13 cm at back of hat, work 2 earflaps.

First earflap: With RS facing, using dpn and color D, pick up and knit 21 sts along edge of hat. Work 7 rows as follows: With WS facing, sl 1, k2, p15, k3. With RS facing, sl 1, k to end. On 8th row begin decreases: sl 1, k2, ssk, work to last 5 sts, k2tog, k3.
Work purl row as before. Continue decreasing on RS rows until 9 sts remain. Purl one row.

Then work the next rows as follows:
Row 1: sl 1, k2, sl 1, k2tog, psso, k3.
Rows 2–5: 4 rows in garter st, continuing to slip first st of each row.
Row 6: sl 1, ssk, k1, k2tog, k1.
Row 7: ssk, k1, k2tog, k1.

Work I-cord on the remaining 3 sts for about 4 in / 10 cm. Break yarn, leaving about 5 in / 12.5 cm. Using a tapestry needle, thread yarn through remaining sts and pull together firmly.

Make second earflap the same.

Weave in loose ends on wrong side of work.

MITTEN INSTRUCTIONS
TERMS USED

m1 right = insert left needle from back to front under the strand between last stitch worked and next stitch on left needle; k this strand through front of the loop
m1 left = insert left needle from front to back under the strand between last stitch worked and next stitch on left needle; k this strand through back of the loop

Cast on 40 (50, 60) sts with color D. Divide onto 3 needles. Join work, being careful not to twist sts. Work Cuff Chart. Work first 4 rounds of Pattern Chart.

Thumb Gusset: For left mitten, work first 2 sts of Round 5 on Pattern Chart; pm (place marker); carrying color B but working with color A, k1, m1 right, k1, m1 left, k1, pm; return to Round 5 of Pattern Chart and work from stitch

6 to end of chart; work as established to end of round. This completes the first row of Thumb Chart. Continue to follow Pattern Chart and Thumb Chart, increasing 1 st after first marker and before second marker every other round as indicated, working increased sts into pattern, until there are 19 sts between markers.

Work until Thumb Chart is completed. On the next round, slip center 17 thumb sts onto holder and cast on 1 st with color C. Work in pattern until hand measures 2 in / 5.5 cm less than desired length, ending with Round 5 or 10 of Pattern Chart.

If you have ended with Round 5, work the following:
Setup Round 1: k2 A, k1 B, *k1 A, k1 B, k7 A, k1 B; repeat from *, ending k1 A, k1 B, k5 A.
Setup Round 2: k3 A, *k1 B, k9 A; repeat from *, ending k1 B, k6 A.

If you have ended with Round 10, work the following:
Setup Round 1: k7 A, k1 B, *k1 A, k1 B, k7 A, k1 B; repeat from *, ending k1 A, k1 B.
Setup Round 2: k8 A, *k1 B, k9 A; repeat from *, ending k1 B, k1 A.

Decrease: *knit to 2 sts before B, k2tog A, k1 B; repeat from *, decreasing before each contrasting st. End round as established. Repeat decrease every other round 4 more times, then every round 5 times. Round 15 is *k2tog color B. Cut yarn and, using a tapestry needle, thread yarn through remaining sts and pull together firmly.

KEY
- ☐ color A
- ◉ color B
- ⊠ color C
- ▨ color D
- · purl these sts

Pattern Chart

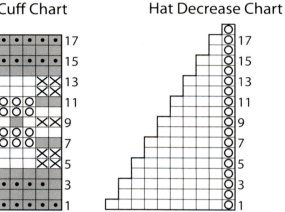

Cuff Chart

Hat Decrease Chart

Thumb Chart

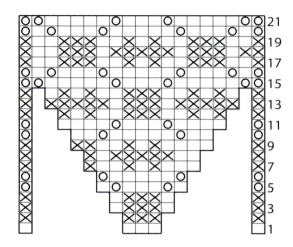

Thumb: With color A, pick up 3 sts at top of thumb hole and 17 sts from holder. Divide on three needles and work in pattern as established until thumb measures ½ in / 1.5 cm less than desired length. Decrease as follows, using color A:
Round 1: *k2, k2tog; repeat from *.
Round 2: knit.
Round 3: *k2tog, repeat from *.

Cut yarn and, using a tapestry needle, thread yarn through remaining sts and pull together firmly.

Right Mitten: Work as for Left Mitten through Round 4 of Pattern Chart. On Round 5 work until 9 sts remain; work Thumb Chart; complete Round 5. Continue Pattern Chart and Thumb Chart to correspond to Left Mitten.

FINISHING
Weave in loose ends on wrong side of work.

For washing instructions read "Caring for Handknits" on page 114.

Icebreaker Hat

Designed by Eric Robinson

"Born" on an icebreaker voyage to the North Pole, this colorful hat with double-knit earflaps will keep you warm in any cold climate. Shown in Colorways I and II.

SIZE: One size fits most adults

FINISHED MEASUREMENTS

CIRCUMFERENCE: 21 in / 53.5 cm

HEIGHT FROM CAST ON TO PEAK: 10 in / 25.5 cm. Hat can be made shorter by eliminating some pattern rows. See chart.

GAUGE: 21 sts and 28 rows over 4 in / 10 cm in 2-color pattern; The hat can be made about 2 in / 5 cm bigger by knitting at a gauge of 19 sts over 4 in / 10 cm.

MATERIALS

YARN: 1 skein of Mountain Mohair in each of 3 colors (A, B, and C), and a small amount in color D

NEEDLES: size 6 US / 4 mm circular needle, 16 in / 40 cm long
dpn, size 6 US / 4 mm

For washing instructions read "Caring for Handknits" on page 114.

BRAIDED EDGING

NB: Your 2 yarns will twist around each other during this process. Don't try to untwist them; simply pull out a healthy amount of yarn and keep going, as they will untwist on the next round.

Using the reverse loop method, cast on 110 sts, alternating colors A and B and always bringing new color *over from the right.* Place marker and join work, being careful not to twist sts.

Round 1: p1 A, p1 B, always bringing new color **under from the left.**

Round 2: p1 A, p1 B, always bringing new color **over from the right.**

Round 3: Repeat round 1.

Round 4: k1 A, k1 B.

Begin chart. On round 5, k54 D, pm (place marker) (center front), k1, pm, k to end. The 5-st repeats marked on the chart are for Rounds 6–22 **only.** From Round 23 on, repeat the entire width of the chart.

Rounds 25 & 26 are a 2-round repeat of the braided edge, beginning with Round 2.

Note where shaping occurs as follows:

Round 40: decrease 2 sts evenly.

Round 47: *k10, [k9, k2tog] 4 times. Repeat from *.

Round 50: *k8, k2tog. Repeat from *, maintaining color pattern.

Round 55: *k7, k2tog. Repeat from *.

Round 61: *k6, k2tog. Repeat from *.

Round 63: *k5, k2tog. Repeat from *.

Round 67: *k4, ssk. Repeat from *.

Round 68: *k3, ssk. Repeat from *.

Round 69: *k2, ssk. Repeat from *.

Round 70: *k1, ssk. Repeat from *.

Round 71: ssk around.

Break yarn, leaving a 9 in / 23 cm end. Thread through remaining stitches and pull snug, but don't finish off yet.

RIGHT EARFLAP

Decide on 2 colors to use for earflaps. With the hat upside down and RS facing, measure 2½ in / 6.5 cm to left of center back; roll the braided edging out and find the purl bumps of Round 4 on the inside of hat (just below color D). Pick up and knit 19 sts in this round, using 2 colors held together and dpn. Turn work. Slip both loops of 1st st together as if to purl. Hold both yarns in the same hand. *With yarns in back, k color A loop of next st with color A; move both yarns to front and p color B loop with color B.

Move yarns to back.* Repeat from * to * until 1 st (2 loops) remains; k both loops together with color A. Turn work. You will now be working 2 contrasting layers at once, one facing you, and one facing away.

Continue as follows: with yarns in front, slip 1st st. Twist the 2 colors around each other to prevent a gap at the edge. *Move yarns to back, k1; move yarns to front, p1.* Repeat from * to * until 1 st remains; k with color A. Turn work. Keeping edge sts in same color, work desired color pattern in this way. I chose 3-row / 2-row stripes; after desired number of rows work next row with the opposite colors.

When 15 rows have been completed, begin shaping: Slip 1st st, then rearrange sts on left needle so you have 2 k sts together and then 2 p sts. With yarn in back, k2tog; with yarn in front, p2tog. Work this decrease at the beginning of every row until 16 sts are left.

Slip the sts onto 2 new dpn, alternating so you have each side of the flap plus one edge st on each needle. With a tapestry needle and the yarn coming from the opposite edge st, join with Kitchener stitch (see Techniques).

Make second earflap to match the first.

FINISHING

NB: Each strand in the braid consists of two same-color pieces of yarn.

Four-strand braids: Cut 2 pieces of yarn in each of 2 colors, about 24 in / 60 cm long. Using a crochet hook, draw them through the end of the

earflap and center them so you have 2 equal strands (two pieces of yarn in each strand) of each color on either side. Lay the strands out so you have 4 strands side by side. *With the outside strand on the right, pass under 2 strands, then reverse direction and go over 1 strand. With the outside strand on the left, pass under 2 strands, then reverse direction and go over 1 strand.* Repeat from * to * until the braid is as long as desired, then tie off. Make a matching one for other side.

The top braid is made with 4 pieces of yarn in each color, each about 14 in / 35.5 cm long. Fold them in half and secure the folded end inside the circle at the top of the hat (then draw up the last sts and fasten tightly). Make the braid as for the earflaps, with 4 pieces of yarn for each strand, and tie off. OR if you prefer, make a tassel, pull the braid yarn through the loop of the tassel and braid to the near end. Then work the loose ends through the top of the hat and weave them inside.

FINISHING

Weave in loose ends on wrong side of work.

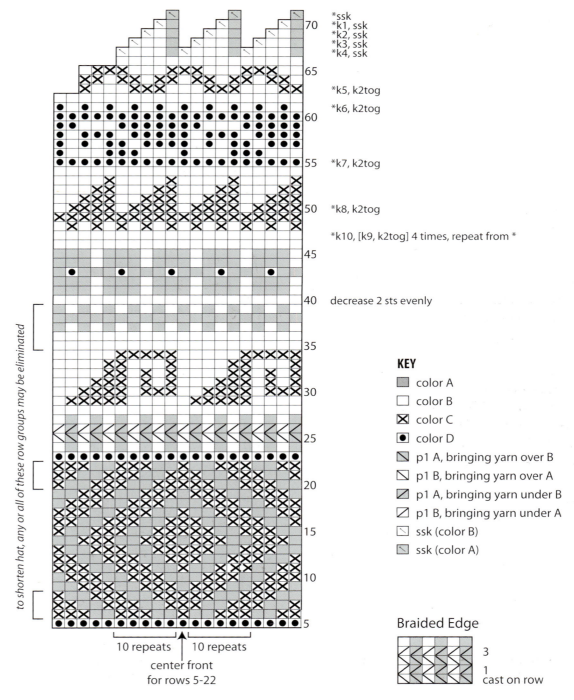

*ssk
*k1, ssk
*k2, ssk
*k3, ssk
*k4, ssk

*k5, k2tog

*k6, k2tog

*k7, k2tog

*k8, k2tog

*k10, [k9, k2tog] 4 times, repeat from *

decrease 2 sts evenly

to shorten hat, any or all of these row groups may be eliminated

10 repeats   10 repeats
center front
for rows 5-22

KEY

- ▩ color A
- ☐ color B
- ☒ color C
- ⊙ color D
- ◨ p1 A, bringing yarn over B
- ◲ p1 B, bringing yarn over A
- ◪ p1 A, bringing yarn under B
- ◩ p1 B, bringing yarn under A
- ◺ ssk (color B)
- ◹ ssk (color A)

Braided Edge

3

1
cast on row

Istanbul Aran

Designed by Melissa Johnson

This sweater is a tribute to Phyllis A. Williams, Melissa's seventh grade teacher at the Robert College Community School in Istanbul. Ms. Williams knit Aran sweaters during her lunch hour, which fascinated Melissa, who wanted to learn her teacher's technique. As Melissa recalls, Ms. Williams did not use charts or a cable needle—just numbers, colored markers, and an understanding of how to manipulate stitches to make the patterns she wanted. The Istanbul Aran is an adaptation of the first sweater Melissa ever knit. It is thanks to Ms. Williams that Melissa began designing sweaters because, although she hadn't yet learned to read knitting patterns, she had learned how to turn ideas into a garment.

SIZES: S (M, L, XL)

FINISHED MEASUREMENTS

CHEST: 40 (44, 48, 52) in / 101.5 (112, 122, 132) cm
LENGTH TO UNDERARM: 12 (14, 16, 18) in / 30.5 (35.5, 40.5, 45.5) cm

GAUGE: 24 sts and 30 rows over 4 in / 10 cm

MATERIALS

YARN: 5 (6, 7, 8) skeins of Wonderfully Woolly or Vermont or Maine Organic OR
9 (11, 13, 14) skeins of Mountain Mohair
NEEDLES: size 5 US / 3.75 mm straight or circular needles AND
size 6 US / 4 mm straight or circular needles AND
size 5 US / 3.75 mm circular needle, 16 in / 40 cm long
NOTIONS: stitch holders

Although the Charts may look daunting, once established they flow in an easy rhythm; and as a bonus, the cables all cross on the same rounds every time!

BACK

Using smaller needle, cast on 121 (135, 147, 159) sts. Work in k1b, p1b twisted rib (both k and p sts are worked into the back on all rows) for 4 rows. Change to larger needles and work setup row for your size as follows. *NB: Read Center Chart Layout from right to left.*

S: k1, work 4 sts in seed st, k1, work Center Chart Layout, k1, 4 seed sts, k1.

M: k1, work 7 sts in seed st, k1, work Chart 5 Right, Center Chart Layout, Chart 5 Left, k1, 7 seed sts, k1.

L: k1, work 9 sts in seed st, k1, work Chart 6 Right, Center Chart Layout, Chart 6 Left, k1, 9 seed sts, k1.

XL: k1, work 11 sts in seed st, Chart 7 Right, Center Chart Layout, Chart 7 Left, k1, 11 seed sts, k1.

Continue in Charts as established until back measures 12 (14, 16, 18) in / 30.5 (35.5, 40.5, 45.5) cm, or desired length to underarm. Bind off 7 (9, 11, 13) sts at the beginning of next two rows.

Working first and last (seam) sts in stockinette st, continue in established patterns until back measures 8 (8½, 9, 9½) in / 20.5 (21.5, 23, 24) cm from bound-off sts, ending with a WS row.

On the next row, bind off 30 (35, 39, 43) sts for right shoulder, work 47 sts and place on holder

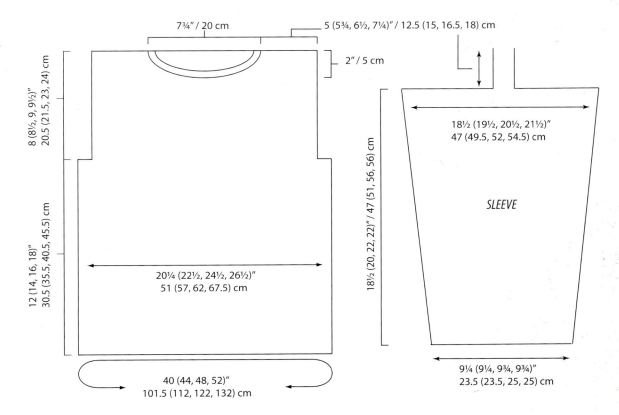

for Back neck, bind off 30 (35, 39, 43) sts for left shoulder.

FRONT

Work same as Back until piece measures 6 (6½, 7, 7½) in / 15 (16.5, 18, 19) cm from bound-off sts, ending with a WS row. On the next row, work across 35 (40, 44, 48) sts for Left Front; place 37 sts on holder for Front neck; join a second ball of yarn and work across remaining 35 (40, 44, 48) sts for Right Front.

Working both sides at once, decrease on the next 5 RS rows as follows: work to 3 sts before neck, k2tog, k1. With second ball, k1, ssk, work to end

of row. Work even until Front measures the same as Back from underarm. Bind off shoulder sts.

SLEEVES *(make 2)*

Using smaller needle, cast on 55 (55, 59, 59) sts and work in k1b, p1b twisted rib (both k and p sts are worked into the back) for 4 rows. Change to larger needle, k1, p2, then begin Chart 3 at the point indicated. Complete Chart 3, work Chart 4 Right, Chart 2, Chart 4 Left, Chart 3 to 3 sts from the end, then p2, k1. *For sizes S and M, work first few chart sts in stockinette st until you have enough to cross the cable.*

KEY

☐ k on RS, p on WS

⊡ p on RS, k on WS

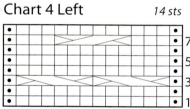 sl 1 to cn and hold in back, k1, k1 from cn

sl 1 to cn and hold in front, k1, k1 from cn

sl 2 to cn and hold in back, k1, k2 from cn

sl 1 to cn and hold in front, k2, k1 from cn

sl 2 to cn and hold in back, k2, k2 from cn

sl 2 to cn and hold in front, k2, k2 from cn

sl 3 to cn and hold in back, k3, k3 from cn

sl 3 to cn and hold in front, k3, k3 from cn

Seed Stitch

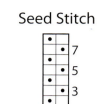

Chart 1 Left   *17 sts*

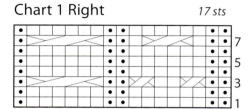

Chart 1 Right   *17 sts*

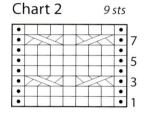

Chart 2   *9 sts*

Chart 3   *10 sts*

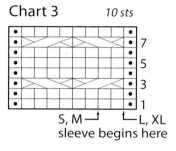

S, M ⌐ ⌐ L, XL
sleeve begins here

Chart 4 Left   *14 sts*

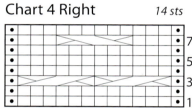

Chart 4 Right   *14 sts*

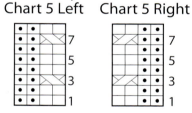

for size M only - 4 sts

Chart 5 Left   Chart 5 Right

for size L only

Chart 6 Left   *8 sts*

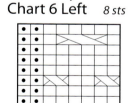

Chart 6 Right   *8 sts*

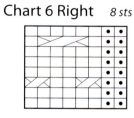

for size XL only

Chart 7 Left   *12 sts*

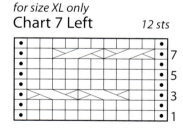

Chart 7 Right   *12 sts*

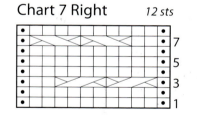

Center Chart Layout for all sizes

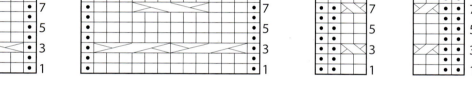

Chart 1 Left	Chart 2	Chart 3	Chart 4 Left	Chart 2	Chart 4 Right	Chart 3	Chart 2	Chart 1 Right

On the 4th row of Chart, increase as follows: k1, m1, work to last sts, m1, k1. Work the increased sts into pattern, always leaving seam st at beginning and end of row and working the same sequence of Charts as for the Back. Increase every 4th row 17 (20, 19, 24) more times, then every 6th row 11 (10, 12, 11) times—111 (117, 123, 129) sts. Continue until sleeve measures 18½ (20, 22, 22) in / 47 (51, 56, 56) cm, or desired length. *NB: If shortening sleeve, be sure to adjust increases accordingly.* Bind off 49 (52, 55, 58) sts on each of the next 2 rows, leaving 13 sts in center for saddle. Work in pattern as established until saddle is the same length as shoulder. Place sts on holder.

FINISHING

Sew side and sleeve seams. Sew sleeves into armholes, then sew saddle to Front and Back shoulders.

NECK

Using smaller 16 in / 40 cm circular needle, place 47 Back neck sts from holder onto needle; pick up and k13 sts for saddle and 12 sts along neck edge; break yarn. Place 37 Front neck sts from holder onto needle; pick up and k12 sts along neck edge and 13 sts for saddle—134 sts. Begin next round with Back neck sts. *NB: Decreases worked in this round should line up over the large cables, to help them lie flat.* Working in twisted rib, [p1, k1] 3 times, [p1, k2tog] 4 times, [p1, k1] 5 times, [p1, ssk] 4 times, [p1, k1] 16 times, [p1, ssk] 4 times, [p1, k1] 6 times, [p1 k2tog] 4 times, p1, k1 to end of round. Work 3 more rounds of twisted rib and bind off.

Weave in loose ends on wrong side of work.

For washing instructions read "Caring for Handknits" on page 114.

Lotus Blossom & Lightning Bolt Hats

Designed by Melissa Johnson

Inspired by classic Nordic skiwear, these fine-gauge hats will keep you warm and elegant on and off the slopes. The Lotus Blossom pattern evolved from wallpaper designs by William Morris, while the graphic work of M. C. Escher inspired the Lightning Bolt.

SIZE: One size fits most adults

FINISHED MEASUREMENTS

CIRCUMFERENCE: 22 in / 56 cm

GAUGE: 30 sts over 4 in / 10 cm

MATERIALS

YARN: 1 skein Spinnery Sock Art Meadow or Forest in Main Color (MC)
1 skein Spinnery Sock Art Meadow or Forest in Contrasting Color (CC)
Waste yarn

NEEDLES: size 0 US / 2 mm AND size 1 US / 2.25 mm circular needles, 16 in / 40 cm long
size C / 2.75 mm crochet hook if desired

KEY

- ☐ Main Color
- ▨ Contrasting Color

LIGHTNING BOLT

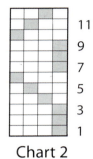

Chart 2

LOTUS BLOSSOM

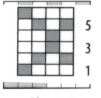

Chart 2

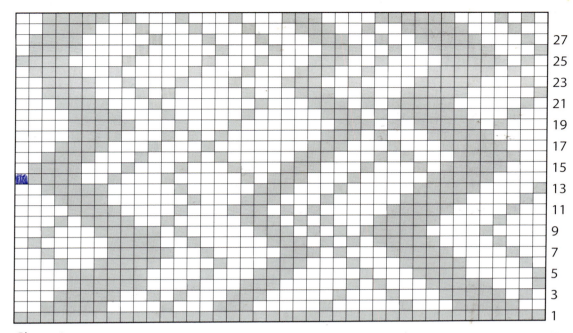

Chart 1

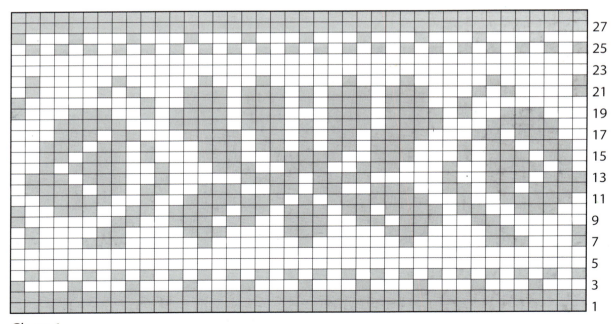

Chart 1

NB: The outside band of the hat is knit first, then the lining, to be sure that the lining is exactly the right length.

Using a provisional method, waste yarn, and larger needle, cast on 160 sts. Join work, being careful not to twist sts, and place marker for beginning of round. Work Chart 1 of Lotus Blossom or Lightning Bolt Pattern. After completing chart, leave sts on needle; pick up sts from provisional cast on with smaller needle. Using MC, purl one round, then knit lining until it measures the same length as outer band. Weave in loose ends, fold lining to inside on purl row, then knit lining and band sts together with larger needle. For Lotus Blossom only, work 2 rounds MC. Work Chart 2 of Lotus Blossom or Lightning Bolt Pattern until hat measures 8 in / 20.5 cm or desired length. With CC, k2tog all around for 2 rounds. Cut yarn, leaving approximately 8 in / 20.5 cm. Using a tapestry needle, thread yarn through remaining sts and pull together firmly. If desired, attach 5 in / 13 cm crocheted chain to top of hat and secure a small tassel to end.

FINISHING

Weave in loose ends on wrong side of work.

For washing instructions read "Caring for Handknits" on page 114.

Switchback Hat

Designed by Melissa Johnson

This Fair Isle hat was designed to showcase the lovely natural shades of Alpaca Elegance. It would work equally well in Cotton Comfort or Sylvan Spirit.

SIZES: S (L)

FINISHED MEASUREMENTS

CIRCUMFERENCE: 18 (21) in / 45.5 (53.5) cm

GAUGE: 24 sts over 4 in / 10 cm

MATERIALS

YARN: 1 skein Main Color (MC), 1 skein each of 3 Contrasting Colors (CC) of Alpaca Elegance

NEEDLES: size 6 US / 4 mm circular needle, 16 in / 40 cm long dpn, size 6 US / 4 mm

Using circular needle and MC, cast on 108 (126) sts. Place marker for beginning of round and join work, being careful not to twist sts. Work Ribbing Chart.

Work 2 (3) repeats of Pattern Chart. Work first 5 rounds of Decrease Chart.

Round 6: k4 MC, ssk with A, k1 A, k1 MC, k1 A, k4 MC, k1 A, k1 MC, k1 A, k2tog A. Continue decreasing in this way, following the Chart. After completing Chart, k2tog around with MC.

Break yarn, leaving 8 in / 20.5 cm. Using a tapestry needle, thread yarn through remaining sts and pull together firmly.

FINISHING
Weave in loose ends on wrong side of work.

For washing instructions read "Caring for Handknits" on page 114.

KEY

- · purl
- ☐ MC
- ☒ color A
- ⊙ color B
- ▨ color C

Ribbing Chart

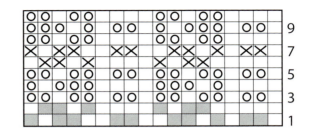

Pattern Chart

Decrease Chart

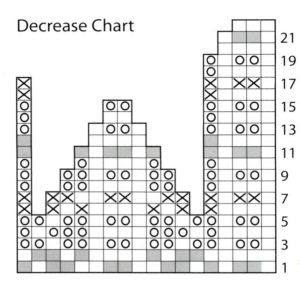

Round 23 - k2tog MC
Round 22 - k1, *k2, k2tog MC; repeat from *

Round 20 - *k3, ssk MC; repeat from *

Round 18 - *k4 MC, k2tog B; repeat from *

1st dec = ssk, 2nd dec = k2tog

Evening Shadows Afghan

Designed by Cap Sease

This afghan highlights the wonderful color variations in the Variegated Green Mountain Green yarn. As the work progresses, you may tire of turning the entire piece each time. Teach yourself to knit backward; you will not have to keep turning the growing afghan and the work will go much faster.

FINISHED MEASUREMENTS

WIDTH: 49 in / 125 cm
LENGTH: 43 in / 110 cm

GAUGE: 18 sts over 4 in / 10 cm

MATERIALS

YARN: 12 skeins of Green Mountain Green Variegated
NEEDLES: size 8 US / 5 mm circular needle, 29 in / 75 cm long

Cast on 120 sts, placing markers after every 10 sts. Knit one row.

Work Base Triangles *(beginning on WS):*
Row 1: p2, turn.
Row 2 & all even rows: knit to end of section (end of row or marker).
Row 3: sl 1, p2, turn.
Row 5: sl 1, p3, turn.
Row 7: sl 1, p4, turn.

Continue as established, purling one more st each WS row until sl 1, p9. Leaving these 10 sts on left needle, sm (slip marker) and repeat base triangle in next section.
Repeat base triangles until you have used up all sts (12 base triangles).

TIER 1 *(RS):*
Work one Right Side Triangle, 11 Left-Leaning Rectangles, one Left Side Triangle.

Right Side Triangle:
Row 1: k2, turn.
Row 2 & all even rows: purl to end, turn.
Row 3: kfb, ssk, turn.
Row 5: kfb, k1, ssk, turn.
Row 7: kfb, k2, ssk, turn.

Continue as established, adding one more k st each RS row before ssk, until kfb, k7, ssk.

Left-Leaning Rectangle:
Row 1: pick up and k 10 sts along side of base triangle (or rectangle in previous tier), turn.
Row 2: purl 10, turn.
Row 3: sl 1, k8, ssk.

Arrows show direction of knitting

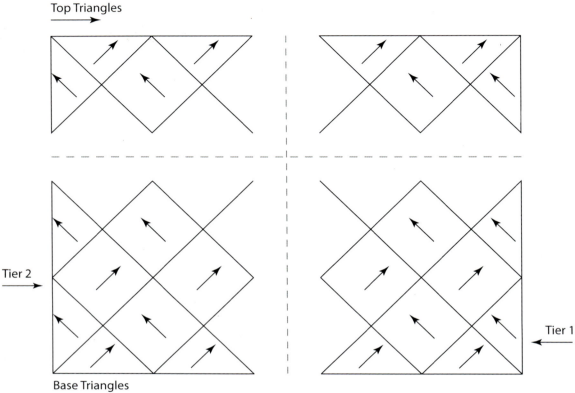

Top Triangles

Tier 2

Base Triangles

Tier 1

Repeat Rows 2 & 3 until 10 sts from left needle have been used up.

Left Side Triangle:
Row 1: pick up and k 10 sts along side of base triangle (or rectangle in previous tier), turn.
Row 2: p2tog, p8, turn.
Row 3 & all further odd rows: sl 1, k to end, turn.
Row 4: p2tog, p7, turn.
Row 6: p2tog, p6, turn.
Row 8: p2tog, p5, turn.

Continue as established, working one fewer p st each WS row to p2tog, turn. One st left on needle.

TIER 2 *(WS):*
Work 12 Right-Leaning Rectangles.
First Right-Leaning Rectangle:
Row 1: pick up and p 9 sts along side of Left Side Triangle, turn.
Row 2: k10, turn.
Row 3: sl 1, p8, p2tog, turn.

Repeat Rows 2 & 3 until 10 sts from right needle have been used up. Then continue across tier with:

Right-Leaning Rectangle:

Row 1: pick up and p 10 sts along side of Left-Leaning Rectangle, turn.

Row 2: k10, turn.

Row 3: sl 1, p8, p2tog, turn.

Repeat Rows 2 & 3 until 10 sts from right needle have been used up. The last rectangle will be picked up on the Right Side Triangle.

//

Work Tiers 1 & 2 four more times, or until afghan measures 2 in / 5 cm less than desired length.

Repeat Tier 1, then:

Work Top Triangles (WS):

Row 1: Pick up and p 9 sts along previous tier, turn.

Row 2 and all even rows: K to end, turn.

Row 3: P2tog, p7, p2tog, turn.

Row 5: P2tog, p6, p2tog, turn.

Row 7: P2tog, p5, p2tog, turn.

Row 9: P2tog, p4, p2tog, turn.

Row 11: P2tog, p3, p2tog, turn.

Row 13: P2tog, p2, p2tog, turn.

Row 15: P2tog, p1, p3tog, turn.

Row 17: P2tog, p3tog, turn.

Row 19: P2tog."

Row 21: p2tog, p2tog, turn.

Row 23: p3tog.

Repeat triangles to end. Break yarn and pull through last st.

FINISHING

Weave in loose ends on wrong side of work.

For washing instructions read "Caring for Handknits" on page 114.

Amanda's Romance

Designed by Eric Robinson during a cross-country train journey (and what's more romantic than that?), this raglan-style wrap is bordered at waist and cuff with an easy lace pattern. Cropped, hip-length, or even longer, this sweater is lovely knit in any of our DK weight yarns. The longer version is shown in Peach Beryl Sylvan Spirit, the cropped version in Winter Beech Cotton Comfort, on Amanda herself.

SIZES: XS (S, M, L, XL, XXL)

FINISHED MEASUREMENTS

CHEST: 33 (36, 38, 41, 44, 47) in / 84 (91.5, 96.5, 104, 112, 119.5) cm

LENGTH TO UNDERARM (CROPPED VERSION): 5½ (6, 7, 8, 9, 10) in / 14 (15, 18, 20.5, 23, 25.5) cm

LENGTH TO UNDERARM (HIP-LENGTH VERSION): *11½ (12, 12½, 13, 13¼, 13½) in / 29 (30.5, 32, 33, 33.5, 34.5) cm*

GAUGE: 21 sts and 32 rows in Baby Cable Pattern, over 4 in / 10 cm

MATERIALS

YARN: Cotton Comfort, Sylvan Spirit or Alpaca Elegance

CROPPED VERSION—5 (5, 6, 6, 7, 7) skeins

HIP LENGTH VERSION—*6 (6, 7, 7, 8, 9) skeins*

NEEDLES: size 7 US / 4.5 mm circular needle, at least 24 in / 60 cm long
dpn, size 7 US / 4.5 mm
size D / 3.25 mm crochet hook

NOTIONS: 4 small stitch holders, 1 or more buttons, as desired

TERMS USED

yo = wrap yarn forward between the needles, all the way around the right needle, and forward again for the next (p) st.

kpk = knit, purl, knit into the same st—double increase

m1 = insert left needle from back to front under the bar between the st just worked and the next st and k this strand through the front

cable = k2tog, but leave on needle; then insert rh needle between the 2 sts just knitted together, and knit the first st again; then slip both sts from needle together

LACE PATTERN—*over 8 sts*

*NB: In this pattern, slip sts **as if to knit.***

Row 1 (WS): sl 1, k1, *yo, p2tog, kpk in next st; repeat from *—12 sts

Row 2: *k3, yo, p2tog; repeat from * once, k2.

Row 3: sl 1, k1, *yo, p2tog, k3; repeat from *.

Row 4: *Bind off 2, yo, p2tog; repeat from *, k2—8 sts

BABY CABLE PATTERN

*NB: In this pattern, slip sts **as if to purl.***

Row 1: knit.

Row 2: sl 1, p to last st, sl 1.

Row 3: k1, p1, k2, p1, *k4, p1, k2, p1; repeat from *, end k1.

Row 4: sl 1, k1, p2, k1, *p4, k1, p2, k1; repeat from *, end sl 1.

Row 5: k1, p1, cable, p1, *k4, p1, cable, p1; repeat from *, end k1.

Row 6: same as Row 4.

Row 7: knit.

Row 8: same as Row 2.

Row 9: k5, *p1, k2, p1, k4; repeat from *, end k1.

KEY

- ☐ k on RS, p on WS
- ⊡ p on RS, k on WS
- ☑ slip st purlwise
- ⧄ cable

Baby Cable Chart

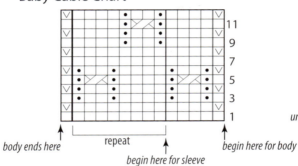

body ends here · repeat · begin here for body

begin here for sleeve

Lace Chart

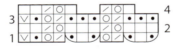

Underarm Chart

continue increases as indicated in pattern

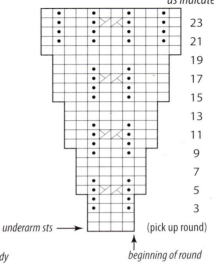

underarm sts → (pick up round)

beginning of round

KEY

- ☐ k on RS, p on WS
- ⊡ p on RS, k on WS
- ☑ slip st knitwise
- Ⓞ yarn over
- ☑ p2 tog
- ⟨•___•⟩ kpk in same st

Row 10: sl 1, p4, *k1, p2, k1, p4; repeat from *, end sl 1.

Row 11: k5, *p1, cable, p1, k4; repeat from *, end k1.

Row 12: same as Row 10.

BODY

Using dpn, cast on 8 sts. Work Lace Pattern for 33 (36, 38, 41, 44, 47) in /84 (91.5, 96.5, 104, 112, 119.5) cm (to measure: stretch slightly so

that picot edge of lace lies flat). Bind off. The sts for the sweater Body are picked up along the slip st edge of the lace in a ratio of approximately 4 sts for every 5 spaces (counting each "peak" and "valley" as a space). Using circular needle and with RS facing, pick up and k174 (190, 198, 214, 230, 246) sts. This is Row 1 of the Baby Cable Pattern. If the number of picked up sts isn't exactly right, you can adjust by increasing or decreasing in Row 2. First and last

sts are selvedge sts and are knit on RS and slipped on WS for a nice edge.

Keeping 1 selvedge st at each edge, work in pattern until sweater measures 5½ (6, 7, 8, 9, 10) in /14 (15, 18, 20.5, 23, 25.5) cm for cropped version, or *11½ (12, 12½, 13, 13¼, 13½) in/29 (30.5, 32, 33, 33.5, 34.5) cm for hip length version*, or desired length to underarm, ending with Row 1 or 7. On next row, divide for Front and Back: sl 1, p49 (54, 56, 61, 66, 70), place last 13 (15, 15, 17, 19, 19) sts worked on a small holder; p87 (95, 99, 107, 115, 123), place last 13 (15, 15, 17, 19, 19) sts worked on a small holder; p36 (39, 41, 44, 47, 51), sl 1, set Body aside.

SLEEVES *(make 2)*
Cast on 8 sts. Work Lace Pattern for a total of 12 (12, 12, 14, 14, 14) repeats; bind off. Sew cast-on end to bound-off end.

With RS facing, and beginning 2 sts before the seam, pick up and k40 (40, 40, 48, 48, 48) sts. Distribute evenly onto 3 dpn. Pm (place marker) after 4th st. The first 4 sts are the underarm sts; on increase rounds, m1 immediately before and after these sts, which are worked as follows:
Rounds 1 & 2: knit (pick up round counts as Rnd 1).
Rounds 3, 4, 6: p1, k2, p1.
Round 5: p1, cable, p1.
Repeat Rounds 1–5 for the underarm sts.

The rest of the Sleeve is worked in Baby Cable Pattern, beginning each round at * (section marked "repeat" on Chart). *Remember that since you are now working in the round, even row sts will now be reversed—knits become purls, and vice* *versa.* Work in pattern, increasing after the first 4 sts and at the end of the round every 5th round 16 (19, 20, 19, 21, 24) times—72 (78, 80, 86, 90, 96) sts. Add new sts to Baby Cable Pattern when you have enough; change to circular needle as needed.

Work even until sleeve measures 16¼ (17, 17½, 17¾, 18, 18¼) in / 41.5 (43, 44.5, 45, 45.5, 46.5) cm, or desired length to underarm. End with Round 2 or 8, working one additional increase after the 2nd st. Place 13 (15, 15, 17, 19, 19) underarm sts on a holder, with the last increased st at center; these underarm sts will later be joined to the underarm sts from the Body.

LACE INSERT PATTERN

This is a modified version of the edging lace.
Row 1 (setup row): knit.
Repeat Rows 2–5 for Pattern.
Row 2 (WS): k2, kpk, k2.
Row 3: p2tog, yo, k3, yo, p2tog.
Row 4: k7.
Row 5: p2tog, yo, bind off 2 sts, yo, p2tog.

Join work:
Row 1: Beginning at right front of Body, *work in pattern to 2 sts before armhole; pm. K2, then k3 from first Sleeve, beginning to the left of the holder (these 5 sts are Row 1 of the Lace Insert Pattern); pm. Work in Baby Cable Pattern as established to 3 sts before end of Sleeve; pm. K3, then k2 from Body; pm.* Repeat from * to * once. Work in pattern to end.
Row 2: *Work in pattern to marker, work Row 2 of Lace Insert Pattern; repeat from * 3 times, work in pattern to end.

Decrease Row 1:
K1, ssk, *work to 2 sts before marker, k2tog, sm (slip marker). Work Insert Pattern Row 3, sm, ssk.* Repeat from * to * 3 times; work to last 3 sts, k2tog, k1.

Continue to work in established patterns, working Decrease Row 1 every 4th row 2 (2, 2, 2, 1, 0) more times. Then dec at each side of Lace Inserts every other row for all sizes, and at neck edge [every 6th row for sizes XS (S, M, L)] 5 (6, 7, 8) times or [every 4th row for sizes XL (XXL)] 11 (13) times. Work neck edge straight while continuing other decreases until you have 1 st in each front. You should have 2 sts for each Sleeve and 18 (20, 22, 24, 28, 30) sts for Back. Dec the last Front st into the lace pattern on the WS. Bind off all sts, working k2tog, k1, k2tog as you bind off the Lace Insertion sts.

FRONT and NECK EDGING

With crochet hook and RS facing, begin at lower left front. Work a crab stitch border: sc (single crochet) in first edge st, then move to the **right** and work another sc (don't untwist the stitch as you go). Continue in this way up the left side, around the neck and down the right side. **For button closure:** At the beginning of the neck shaping on the right side chain a few sts for a button loop, then sc in the same st. Continue to end. **For tie closure:** Attach crochet ties or ribbons to both edges at the beginning of the neck shaping.

FINISHING

Weave underarm seams. Weave in loose ends on wrong side of work.

For washing instructions read "Caring for Handknits" on page 114.

Retro Ribbed Turtleneck

A classic turtleneck pullover, featuring a seed stitch vertical stripe, is a great way to show off a classic yarn. The pattern is offered in a range of sizes for him or her. Shown in Storm Cotton Comfort.

SIZES: S (M, L, XL, XXL)

FINISHED MEASUREMENTS

CHEST: 38 (41½, 45, 48½, 51) in / 96.5 (105.5, 114.5, 123, 129.5) cm

LENGTH TO UNDERARM: 13½ (14, 14½, 15, 15½) in / 34.5 (35.5, 37, 38, 39.5) cm

GAUGE: 24 sts and 32 rows over 4 in / 10 cm, using larger needle

MATERIALS

YARN: 8 (9, 9, 10, 11) skeins of Cotton Comfort, Sylvan Spirit, or Alpaca Elegance

NEEDLES: size 5 US / 3.75 mm circular needle, 29 in / 80 cm long AND
size 4 US / 3.5 mm circular needle, 16 in / 40 cm long
2 straight needles, any size
size E / 3.5 mm crochet hook

NOTIONS: 1 large, 4 small stitch holders

Using larger needle, cast on 230 (250, 270, 290, 310) sts. Place marker for beginning of round and join work, being careful not to twist sts. Work Rib Pattern as follows:
Round 1: *k4, p1; repeat from *.
Round 2: *p1, k4; repeat from *.

Repeat these two Rounds until piece measures 13½ (14, 14½, 15, 15½) in / 34.5 (35.5, 37, 38, 39.5) cm, or desired length to underarm.

Divide for Armholes: Work across 109 (119, 128, 138, 148) sts; bind off 12 (12, 14, 14, 14) sts. Work across 103 (113, 121, 131, 141) sts for Front; bind off 12 (12, 14, 14, 14) sts (half at end of Front and half at beginning of Back). Place sts for Front on large holder.

Front and Back yokes are worked back and forth, maintaining 3 sts at each end of row in stockinette st.

The Rib Pattern will now be:
Row 1: *k4, p1; repeat from *.
Row 2: *p4, k1; repeat from *.

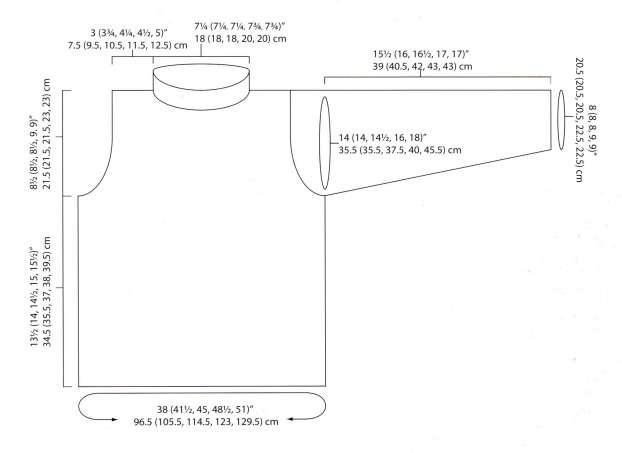

3 (3¾, 4¼, 4½, 5)"
7.5 (9.5, 10.5, 11.5, 12.5) cm

7¼ (7¼, 7¼, 7¾, 7¾)"
18 (18, 18, 20, 20) cm

15½ (16, 16½, 17, 17)"
39 (40.5, 42, 43, 43) cm

20.5 (20.5, 20.5, 22.5, 22.5) cm
8 (8, 8, 9, 9)"

14 (14, 14½, 16, 18)"
35.5 (35.5, 37.5, 40, 45.5) cm

8½ (8½, 8½, 9, 9)"
21.5 (21.5, 21.5, 23, 23) cm

13½ (14, 14½, 15, 15½)"
34.5 (35.5, 37, 38, 39.5) cm

38 (41½, 45, 48½, 51)"
96.5 (105.5, 114.5, 123, 129.5) cm

BACK

Work across 103 (113, 121, 131, 141) sts of Back as follows:
Row 1: k3, work in established Rib to last 3 sts, k3.
Row 2 (WS): p3, work in established Rib to last 3 sts, p3.
On the next row (RS), decrease as follows: k2, ssk, work in pattern to last 4 sts, k2tog, k2. Continue to decrease in this manner every RS row for a total of 12 (12, 14, 15, 17) times—79 (89, 93, 101, 107) sts. Work even until piece

measures 8½ (8½, 8½, 9, 9) in / 21.5 (21.5, 21.5, 23, 23) cm from dividing round, ending with WS row.

Shape Shoulders: Work short rows as follows.
Row 1: Work to last 6 (8, 9, 9, 10) sts; turn.
Row 2: sl 1, work to last 6 (8, 9, 9, 10) sts; turn.
Row 3: sl 1, work to last 12 (16, 16, 18, 20) sts; turn.
Row 4: sl 1, work to last 12 (16, 16, 18, 20) sts; turn.

Row 5: sl 1, work to last 18 (23, 25, 27, 30) sts; turn.
Bind off 43 (43, 43, 47, 47) sts for back neck. Place remaining 18 (23, 25, 27, 30) sts for each shoulder on separate holders.

FRONT

Work same as Back until piece measures 6 (6, 6, 6½, 6½) in / 15 (15, 15, 16.5, 16.5) cm, ending with a WS row. On the next row, work across 26 (31, 33, 35, 38) sts for Left Front and place on a holder; bind off 27 (27, 27, 31, 31) sts for neck; work across remaining 26 (31, 33, 35, 38) sts for Right Front.

Right Front:
Row 1 (WS): p3, work in pattern to last 3 sts, p3.
Row 2: k2, ssk, work to last 3 sts, k3.
Repeat these 2 rows 7 more times—18 (23, 24, 27, 30) sts. Continue in pattern, maintaining 3 stockinette sts at each end of row, until piece measures the same as Back from dividing round, ending with a WS row.

Work short rows as follows:
Row 1: Work to last 6 (8, 9, 9, 10) sts; turn.
Row 2: sl 1, work to neck edge.
Row 3: Work to last 12 (16, 16, 18, 20) sts; turn.
Row 4: sl 1, work to neck edge.
Place all sts on a holder.

Left Front:
Work to correspond to Right Front. Decreases will be as follows:
Row 1 (WS): p3, work in pattern to last 3 sts, p3.
Row 2: k3, work in pattern to last 4 sts, k2tog, k2.
After decreases are complete, work until piece measures the same as Right Front from dividing round, ending with a RS row.

Short rows are worked the same as for Right Front, except that Rows 1 & 3 are WS rows, Rows 2 & 4 are RS rows. When short rows are complete, place all sts on a holder.

Join shoulders using the three-needle bind off (see Techniques).

TURTLENECK

With RS facing, using smaller needle and beginning at left shoulder, pick up and k16 sts along left neck edge, pm; pick up and k the 27 (27, 27, 31, 31) bound-off sts at front neck, pm; pick up and k16 sts along right neck edge, pm; pick up and k the 43 (43, 43, 47, 47) bound-off sts at back neck, pm—102 (102, 102, 110, 110) sts. Knit one round. On the next round, decrease 1 st at the 4 corners of neck edge, removing markers to make decs: k to one st before marker, ssk, pm; k to one st before marker, k2tog, pm, k to one st before marker, k2tog, pm, k to one st before marker, ssk, pm. Knit 3 rounds.

Decrease Round 2: k to 2 sts before marker, ssk; k to 2 sts before marker, k2tog, k to 2 sts before marker, k2tog, k to 2 sts before marker, ssk—94 (94, 94, 102, 102) sts. Leave the last marker in place; the others can be removed.
Work 5 rounds k1, p1 rib. On the 5th round of rib, increase 1 (1, 1, 3, 3) sts evenly.
Turn work, and begin Rib Pattern stitch on the *inside* of turtleneck. Work until pattern st measures 3½ in / 9 cm, or desired length. Decrease 1 st at end of last round.

Work seed st:
Round 1: *k1, p1; repeat from *.
Round 2: *p1, k1; repeat from *.
Repeat Round 1. Bind off loosely in pattern.

SLEEVES *(make 2)*
Using larger needle, cast on 48 (48, 48, 53, 53) sts and work back and forth in Rib Pattern as follows:
Row 1 (WS): *p4, k1; repeat from *, end p3.
Row 2: *k4, p1; repeat from *, end k3.
Repeat these rows 2 more times.
Increase Row: k2, kfb, work to last 4 sts; kfb, k3.
Work the increased sts in stockinette st; when 5 increases have been made, work these sts into Rib Pattern. Increase every 6th row 14 (14, 16, 17, 17) times, then every 4th row 3 times—84 (84, 88, 95, 95) sts.

Continue in Rib Pattern until sleeve measures 15½ (16, 16½, 17, 17) in / 39 (40.5, 42, 43, 43) cm, or desired length to underarm. Bind off 6 (6, 6, 7, 7) sts on each of the next 2 rows. On next RS row decrease as follows: k2, ssk, work to last 4 sts, k2tog, k2. Work decreases every other row 14 (14, 15, 15, 15) more times—42 (42, 44, 49, 49) sts. Work 7 (7, 7, 4, 4) rows even; bind off 2 sts on each of the next 4 rows. Bind off all sts.

FINISHING
Sew sleeves into armholes. Sew sleeve seams. Weave in loose ends on wrong side of work.

For washing instructions read "Caring for Handknits" on page 114.

Resources

GREEN MOUNTAIN SPINNERY YARNS

For best results with our patterns, use the Green Mountain Spinnery yarns specified. Our yarns are listed below.

ALPACA ELEGANCE in 5 colors
2-ply, 50% New England–grown alpaca / 50% fine wool
2 oz/58 g skein, approximately 180 yds/165 m

COTTON COMFORT in 14 colors
2-ply, 80% fine wool/20% Organic Cotton
2 oz/58 g skein, approximately 180 yds/165 m

GREEN MOUNTAIN GREEN in 3 colors
2-ply, 40% kid mohair/60% fine wool
2 oz/58 g skein, approximately 120 yds/110 m

MAINE ORGANIC in 3 colors
2-ply, 100% Certified Organic Wool grown in Maine and Certified by Maine Organic Farmers. Processing Certified by Vermont Organic Farmers.
4 oz/116 g skein, approximately 250 yds/228 m

MOUNTAIN MOHAIR in 34 colors
Single ply, 30% yearling mohair/70% wool
2 oz/58 g skein, approximately 140 yds/128 m

NEW MEXICO ORGANIC in 2 colors
2-ply, 100% Certified Organic Wool grown in New Mexico and Certified by the New Mexico Organic Commodities Commission. Processing Certified by Vermont Organic Farmers.
2 oz/58 g skein, approximately 180 yds/165 m

MOHAIR

It's mohair that creates the soft, fuzzy halo in our Green Mountain Green and Mountain Mohair yarns. Mohair comes from the fleece of the Angora goat, an animal named for the ancient Turkish city of Ankara and prized through the ages for its luxurious fiber. The term *mohair* is thought to derive from the Arabic word *mukhayya*, which means "cloth of bright hair from a goat."

Angoras are generally sheared twice a year and yield, on average, a 3- to 5-pound fleece. Fiber from the youngest goats—kid mohair—is the softest; fiber becomes coarser as the animal ages. The Spinnery uses kid mohair in Green Mountain Green and fine mohair from yearlings in Mountain Mohair. We use about 2,000 pounds of mohair a year, equal to the fleece of approximately 600 goats!

SPINNERY SOCK ART—MEADOW
2-ply, 50% kid mohair/50% fine wool
Approximately 3½ oz/100 g skein, 400 yds/365 m

SPINNERY SOCK ART—FOREST
2-ply, 70% fine wool/30% TENCEL lyocell
Approximately 3½ oz/100 g skein, 400 yds/365 m

SYLVAN SPIRIT in 10 colors
Single ply, 50% fine wool/50% TENCEL lyocell
2 oz/58 g skein, approximately 180 yds/165 m

WONDERFULLY WOOLLY in 20 colors

2-ply, 100% New England–grown wool

4 oz/100 g skein, approximately 250 yds/228 m

VERMONT ORGANIC

2-ply 100% Certified Organic Wool, Vermont grown. Farm and
processing Certified by Vermont Organic Farmers.

4 oz/100 g skein, approximately 250 yds/228 m

YARN OVER in 5 colors

2-ply heavy worsted, a blend of wool, mohair and other natural fibers

4 oz/100 g skein, approximately 155 yds/142 m

*NB: Our yarns are versatile and can be knit at different gauges depending on
needle size. For example, Mountain Mohair makes a firm fabric on US size
3/3.25 mm needles for mittens and a soft, drapey fabric on US size 9/5.5 mm.*

CARING FOR HANDKNITS

Spinnery yarns are softer and more beautiful after being gently washed by
hand. Garments knit with natural-fiber yarns are easy to care for and
wash. Gentle hand-washing continues to soften the fibers and will greatly
extend their life. Choose a mild or vegetable oil–based soap, or try one of
the many specialty wool-wash products available. A mild dishwashing liq-
uid without enzymes is also suitable.

Fill a deep sink, basin, or your washing machine with enough lukewarm water to cover the items to be washed. Add a small amount of soap
and agitate the water to make a sudsy bath. If you are using your washing
machine, *turn the machine off now*. Immerse the garment, gently squeezing
the water through until it is completely saturated. Soak for 10–20 minutes.
Drain the water from the sink, or spin out the water from your washing
machine using the gentle cycle in short bursts as needed. Rinse in the
same way, with clean lukewarm water. Lay the item flat to dry on a screen
or heavy towel and carefully shape to measurements.

ORGANIC YARNS

In offering our Certified Organic yarns, we celebrate the special care given by
sheep breeders to their land and animals. We are pleased to have developed and
to provide certified organic processing as we wash, card, and spin the fibers
from these Vermont, Maine, and New Mexico flocks. Annual inspections by state
authorities set the standards for both the fibers and the processing.

Livestock are not confined but are raised using humane and organic methods;
they graze on pastures free of chemical additives and receive only organically
grown feed. Strict standards also apply for treating flocks for pathogens.

In accordance with Vermont standards for organic processing, we use non-
petroleum-based soaps and organic spinning oils in preparing the fibers, and
bio-oils to lubricate our spinning and plying machines. We continually strive to
improve these products; for example, we have recently ensured that the citric
acid preservative in our spinning oil is not synthetic.

By purchasing these yarns, you partner with the farmers and with us in pre-
serving healthy soil, healthy animals, and a healthy planet. In addition, it is our
expectation that people with chemical sensitivities may use and wear these
yarns with comfort.

KNITTING BOOKS

Budd, Ann. *The Knitter's Handy Book of Sweater Patterns*. Loveland, CO:
Interweave Press, 2004.

Editors of *Vogue Knitting Magazine*. *Vogue Knitting: The Ultimate Knitting
Book*. New York: Sixth and Spring Books, 2002.

Gibson-Roberts, Priscilla. *Knitting in the Old Way*. Loveland, CO:
Interweave Press, 1985.

Square, Vicki. *The Knitter's Companion: Expanded and Updated.* Loveland, CO: Interweave Press, 2006.

Walker, Barbara G. *A Treasury of Knitting Patterns.* 1968. Pittsville, WI: Schoolhouse Press, 1998.

———. *A Second Treasury of Knitting Patterns.* Pittsville, WI: Schoolhouse Press, 1998.

Wilson, Margaret Klein, and the Green Mountain Spinnery. *The Green Mountain Spinnery Knitting Book: Contemporary and Classic Patterns.* Woodstock, VT: The Countryman Press, 2003.

GREENSPUN PROCESS

In the mid-1990s, the Spinnery switched to non-petroleum-based biodegradable soaps for scouring fibers. We also developed a spinning oil formula based on organic canola oil for processing fiber. These gentle and ecologically safe practices became our *GREENSPUN* processing method. Used for all our *GREENSPUN* and Certified Organic yarns, these methods enhance the unique qualities of the natural fibers. Customers with chemical sensitivities have been relieved to find and are enthusiastic about our chemical-free yarns.

ONLINE RESOURCES FOR KNITTERS:

A remarkable Web site, www.KnittingHelp.com presents videos and descriptions of a vast array of knitting techniques. This is almost as good as having a knitting teacher on call.

Ravelry.com is an online social-networking site. Knitters share information about patterns, yarns, and resources. It is a great way to experience the international community of knitters.

MORE INFORMATION
ABOUT WORKER-OWNED COOPERATIVES:

The Cooperative Development Institute, 1 Sugarloaf Street, South Deerfield, MA 01373, 1-877-NECOOPS, 413-665-1271, www.cdi.coop.

Vermont Employee Ownership Center, 41 Main Street, P.O. Box 546, Burlington, VT 05402, 802-861-6611, www.veoc.org.

FARMS AND FIBER PEOPLE who have helped with this project and produce excellent yarns and products:

Greenwood Hill Farm
Andrea and Tom Colyer
P.O. Box 534, Hubbardston, MA 01452
Natural-colored merino yarns and knitting patterns

IBIWISI Alpaca
Cathy McKenny
Westminster, VT 05158
www.ibiwisialpacas.com
Alpaca fibers and yarns, alpaca breeding stock, and pets

Long Ridge Farm
Jack and Nancy Zeller
Westmoreland, NH 03467

www.longridgefarm.com

CVM Romeldale fleeces and yarns, naturally dyed yarn and Earthhues Natural Dye kits

Mountain Vewe Coopworths

Richard and Marianne Dube

P.O. Box 48, West Newbury, VT 05085

Fleeces and hand-dyed yarns

Noon Family Sheep Farm

Jean Noon

Springvale, ME 04083

www.jeannoon.com

Certified Organic Lamb

Snow Star Farm

Loranne Carey Block

Loveren Mill Road, Antrim, NH 03440

snowstar@tds.net

Hand-dyed yarns and knitting kits

This and That Farm

Donna Herrick

2212 Tinmouth Road, Danby, VT 05739

www.thisandthatfarm.com

Cormo fleeces and yarn

Vermont Shepherd Cheese

David and Yesenia Ielpi Major

281 Patch Farm Road, Putney, VT 05346

www.vermontshepherd.com

Award-winning sheep's-milk cheese

ALPACA

Alpacas are camelids, native to the Andes Mountains of South America. They are most common throughout the highlands of southern Peru, Bolivia, and Chile. Like their llama cousins, they have been domesticated for about five thousand years.

Valued for their extraordinary fleece, alpacas come in a remarkable range of colors, from bright white to deep black, with many shades of brown and grey between. Alpacas were first imported to the United States in 1984 and have adapted well to the New England climate. The availability of locally grown alpaca fleece has increased as many fiber enthusiasts have discovered the joy of working with this luxury fiber.

In 1998, the diversity of colors available inspired us to design a line of naturally colored *GREENSPUN* yarn, Alpaca Elegance, a blend of New England–grown alpaca and fine wool.

ACKNOWLEDGMENTS

The Green Mountain Spinnery is the work of many minds and hands; likewise this book has many authors.

Margaret Atkinson, Maureen Clark, Melissa Johnson, Judy "Eric" Robinson, and Catherine "Cap" Sease provided the core work of this project, designing and knitting patterns, doing technical editing, and writing the text. All schematics are by Eric Robinson. Melissa created the art that is featured on the cover.

David Ritchie, Patty Blomgren, Marshall "Laurie" Gilbert, and Gail Haines supported us in countless ways throughout this project, along with the wonderful and tolerant Spinnery workers Tedd Kapinos, Betsy MacIsaac, Sarah Waggener, Ingrid Cabrey, and Sheila McLane.

Thanks to Claire Wilson and Libby Mills for their insights and contributions to the manuscript.

We are so grateful to photographer Marti Stone for joining us on this project. Her great appreciation of people and their work and her amazing ability to focus on the beauty in our everyday reality shine through. Technical photo assistance was provided by Colin Stone and Scott Rocknak.

Many thanks to location owners and their families, who helped us to showcase our designs and the New England landscape: The Major family at the Major Farm, Cathy McKenny and IBIWISI Alpacas, and Libby Mills at her home, all in Westminster, Vermont; Tedd Kapinos at the fine fibre farm in Wethersfield, Vermont; Nancy Zeller at Long Ridge Farm, Westmoreland, New Hampshire; Jean Noon at the Noon Family Farm in Springvale, Maine; and Brien and Emily Davis at Hope Orchards in Hope, Maine.

Thanks to our amazing sweater models and their families: Kristy, Kelly, and Haylie Clark; Riley Jacobs; Lana, Yesenia, and David Ilepi Major; Austin Lee Ilepi Major; Jazzlyn Rae Molloy and Robyn O'Brien; Phelan Muller; Noah and Katy Richardson; Phoebe, Leo, and Jim Rodda; Owen and Malcolm Toleno; Susie Webster-Toleno; Seth Peters; Tedd Kapinos and Gracie; Ames Curtis; Michaela Stone and Chantey; Paula Huntsman

and Grady; Antoinette Nelson; Mia Cobourn; Will Jurek; Hillary Steinau; Conrad, Stryker, Scott, and Lucinda A. Rocknak; Anneli Skaar Rocknak; Kate and Anna Rich; Fletcher Davis; Elizabeth VanLonkhuyzen; Alexandra Lawrence; William White Curtis; Julia, Cooper, and Amy Russell; Amanda Cramer; Paige and Reid Chester; Emma Conover; and Lucy O'Brien.

At the New Hampshire Sheep and Wool Festival: Loranne Block of Snow Star Farm; Jim and Andrea Colyer of Greenwood Hill Farm; Marianne and Suzanne Dube of Mountain Vewe Coopworths; and Donna Herrick of This and That Farm. We thank them for allowing us to photograph them and their booths at such a busy time.

Thanks to model knitters Patty Blomgren, Linda Fawcett, Amanda Cramer, and the Spinnery product development team.

Special thanks to Kate Gilbert for her magic spreadsheet and to Celia Bohannon for her keen eye and sympathetic ear.

Thanks to our agent, Linda Roghaar, and to Lisa Sacks and Kermit Hummel at The Countryman Press for all their support.

PATTERN INDEX

PAGE 16

PAGE 19

PAGE 21

PAGE 21

PAGE 25

PAGE 28

PAGE 31

PAGE 34

PAGE 36

PAGE 40

PAGE 42

PAGE 46

PAGE 48

PAGE 50

PAGE 53

PAGE 56

PAGE 59

PAGE 62

PAGE 64

PAGE 66

PAGE 69

PAGE 71

PAGE 74

PAGE 77

PAGE 80

PAGE 84

PAGE 86

PAGE 86

PAGE 89

PAGE 92

PAGE 96

PAGE 99

PAGE 101

PAGE 104

PAGE 108